MONIQUE ROMERO

The Salvation Walk

A Journey of Faith

THIS BOOK IS DEDICATED TO
MY HEAVENLY FATHER:
THANK YOU LORD FOR YOUR EVERLASTING LOVE,
THANK YOU FOR WASHING ME CLEAN,
THANK YOU GOD FOR NEVER LEAVING OR FORSAKING ME,
THANK YOU FOR GIVING ME A NEW LIFE,
THANK YOU FOR GIVING ME YOUR SPIRIT TO DWELL WITHIN.

Contents

Foreword   ii

Acknowledgments   iii

Introduction   1

 1 Discovering Your Defining Moment   7

 2 Understanding God's Love and Purpose   10

 3 The Power of Full Surrender   14

 4 Walking with God Daily   18

 5 Navigating Life's Challenges with Faith   22

 6 Transformation Through the Word   26

 7 Building a closer Relationship with God   32

 8 Freedom Through Christ   43

 9 Finding Purpose and Direction   53

10 The Joy of Fellowship and Community   66

11 Living Set Apart for God   74

12 Preparing for Spiritual Battle   83

13 Embracing Daily Renewal and Growth   93

14 Conclusion Walking Forward in Faith   113

15 Resources: 120

16 Table of Contents Reflection   121

Foreword

THE SALVATION WALK
 A
 JOURNEY OF FAITH!
 BY
 MONIQUE ROMERO

ARE YOU READY?

Acknowledgments

I want to thank My children for encouraging me and being there for me always, All of my family who has always supported me from afar, My circle who has been there through all the ups and downs also the closest people who let me read or go over things with them you all know who you are, The ones who love me unconditionally and sometimes stay up late listening to me talk even when they are tired lol, and my church family new and old you all mean more to me than you know! Thank you all for helping spark my shine! Love you all!

Introduction

The call to a transformed life

I often, find myself reflecting, on how many people struggle to find their way back to Christ. They feel uncertain about where to start or how to take those first steps. Even new believers can find themselves wondering, "What comes next?" They may ask where to begin reading the Bible, which church to attend, or who to seek out for fellowship and guidance. You've likely found yourself pondering these same questions.

Let me assure you that each person's walk with Christ is unique. We all grow at our own pace and we all learn in different ways. Though we are all headed toward the same destination the paths we take to get there may vary. Along the way, there will be obstacles, detours, and seasons of construction that can feel like roadblocks. But remember, God is always at work, redirecting our steps one day at a time, one step at a time.

I wrote this book to support you on your journey of faith. I hope, to help you grow in your way, realizing that every testimony and process is unique. May this book inspire you to fully embrace your walk with God, seeking all He has for you with a fresh perspective and insight.

The first step I encourage you to take is to fully surrender to return to the source of your life, the One who loved you first. Lay everything before Him: your past, your sins, your hurts, your fears, and all your worries. Give Him everything this world has placed upon you until there is nothing left of yourself, and all that remains is Him. When you empty yourself, you create space for God to fill you with His presence.

Next, come before Him with a repentant heart. Confess your sins and ask God to forgive you, to cleanse you, and to set you free. Thank Him for sending His Son to die on the cross for you, and if you believe that Jesus rose from the dead to give you new life, ask Him to fill you with the Holy Spirit. Seek a deep hunger for the things of God and a holy boldness to share the gospel of Jesus Christ. Declare that you are saved, born again, and forgiven, knowing that your eternal destination is secure because Jesus is now in your heart, guiding your steps and leaving nothing to chance.

If you have prayed this prayer of salvation, I want to congratulate you and welcome you to the family of Christ. This is your new beginning the new you has arrived, and the old is gone.

Now that you have emptied yourself and fully surrendered to being reborn, you are ready to receive all God has for you. Let His Spirit guide you, no longer allowing your flesh to lead.

Remember, this journey will not always be easy, The road ahead will have trials and tribulations, and there will be storms that come your way. The enemy will try to reclaim the old you and your flesh may attempt to pull you back expect these challenges

2

and more, because they will come. But know this God is with you! Despite all these struggles, this walk with Him is worth every step.

Believe me when I say I've been where you are now, or where you've been at some point in your life. This journey is a process of growth The more prepared you are the less power the enemy your flesh or anyone else will have to come between you and our Heavenly Father. When you are firmly planted on the foundation of His love nothing can move you, Once you stand secure in His love, no one and nothing can take it away from you.

When we return to our first love, God gives us more than we could ever offer Him abundantly. Yes, we go through seasons of trials, loss, and pain. But God equips us to face everything this world throws at us, and He strengthens us through each season, preparing us for whatever lies ahead. In His Word, He shows us how to live and follow Him. But beyond the words, it's about having a true relationship with Him. This means abiding in Him, spending time with Him, speaking to Him daily, crying out to Him, worshiping Him, and building a deep connection. As you do this, the Holy Spirit, who dwells within you, will guide you as your faith, obedience, belief, trust, and love for the One who first loved you, continue to grow.

As I mentioned before, it all begins with surrender. From there, you can receive the understanding that everyone learns, thinks, and acts differently. When you allow God to be your guide and trust in His ways, your relationship with Him will grow stronger than ever. This growth happens one day at a time, one step at a time. Don't rush the process and don't doubt what He is doing within you, even when you don't see or feel it. He is always at work, performing miracles daily even the very breath you take and the sunshine that warms you are miracles of His creation.

If you are still reading this, be proud of yourself for wanting to know more about our loving Father, desiring to love Him as He loves you, and seeking more than what this world offers. It's a step-by-step journey and that's okay don't be hard on yourself if your growth doesn't seem as fast as you'd like or if you feel you're not where you thought you'd be by now. Remember, we are all different, and that is perfectly fine. God sees your growth, and that is what truly matters.

Scripture says:

John 14:15 (NKJV): *If you love me, keep my commandments.*

If we become comfortable with something in our life that God, calls sin we are not obeying him.

Have you ever asked yourself, "Am I truly at peace with God?" Are you battling against sin, or are you resisting God? Whichever one you make peace with, you will find yourself at war with the other I know I don't want to be at war with God, do you? I would much rather find peace with the One who created me and trust Him to fight the battle against sin, step by step, every day.

Scripture says:

Exodus 19:5 (NKJV): *Now, therefore if you will indeed obey My voice and keep my covenant then you shall be a special treasure to me above all people for all the earth is mine.*

We are His treasures He calls us special and beautiful. Yet, how often do we fail to see ourselves that way? Far too many times isn't it?

Scripture says:

Deuteronomy 11:1 (NKJV): *Therefore you shall love the Lord your God and keep His charge, His statutes, His judgments, and His commandments always.*

Jesus tells us that just as the Father loves Him He loves us. Ask yourself, "How am I showing my love to Him? Am I truly expressing my love for Him in my daily life?"

Scripture says:

2 Corinthians 10:5 (NKJV): *Casting down arguments and every high thing that exalts itself against the knowledge of God, bringing every thought into captivity to the obedience of Christ.*

He instructs us in His Word to obey Him and to honor our Father and Mother. This is the first commandment with a promise that He will be with us and grant us a long life on earth. We are called to be living, breathing sacrifices, dying to the flesh each day, and following Him, allowing the Holy Spirit to guide and take over our lives continually.

Scripture says:

Revelation 14:12 (NKJV): *Here is the patience of the saints here are those who keep the commandments of God and the faith of Jesus.*

Ask yourself, Are you truly following God? Are, you lacking anything, in your obedience to Christ? Through Christ, we receive His grace, mercy, love, and the calling to obedience a faith that reaches every nation for His name's sake. Obeying God's commands brings righteousness into our hearts it's, through obedience to His truth that He delivers us from death to eternal life.

1

Discovering Your Defining Moment

When we choose a life built on God's truths, not the world's ways, we avoid the path of destruction. But if we follow man's perspective over God's, we will surely stumble. Ask yourself, "Do I love God?" If the answer is yes, then you will strive to obey Him, even when it is difficult, when the storms rage, when people turn against you, and when you lose those you thought would always be there.

You might find yourself in situations where people you thought were your friends turn against you. Remember, Jesus warned us that we would face troubles in this world, and indeed, people hated Him when He walked the earth. Yet, He is always with us. The closer we draw to Him, the more we see His direction in our lives.

We are not saved by our works but by our faith, yet it's important to remember that faith without works is dead. Our obedience to our Father reflects our love for Him, how close we are to Him, and how we honor praise and fellowship with Him. Obeying Him is not a mere request or favor but a command.

As we follow His commands, even when battles arise and challenges seem insurmountable, our obedience reveals our alignment with God's righteousness. He will guide you, taking care of all your needs and making a way where there seems to be none. He gives us what we ask for and so much more abundantly an everlasting life filled with His love, joy, peace, and happiness.

Living a life focused on His truth, rather than following the world's views, keeps us from the path of destruction. you continue with a mindset aligned with human ways over God's, you risk falling. Ask yourself, "Do I truly love God?" If your answer, is yes, then you will obey Him even when it gets hard, when the storms come, when people stand against you, and when you lose those you love.

In the past, people sacrificed animals, but today, we sacrifice ourselves. We place ourselves on the altar, in full surrender dying daily to the flesh and living in His Holy Spirit, with His grace, mercy, and love. Our obedience is about following Him with everything we have. If you notice changes in your behavior, show your obedience through your actions. Many stories in the Bible describe how God asked people to leave everything and follow Him, and those who were obedient were richly rewarded. While we should seek to please Him, not just to gain rewards, God, does indeed bless obedience.

We cannot remove sin by ourselves, but God can. We can choose to obey His words or ignore them. The Bible teaches us about good and evil, guiding us in our walk. God is always present, even when we fall, extending His mercy, grace, love, judgment, and conviction. The story of Hezekiah is an example of obedience. During a time when Judah was sinful and worshiping idols, Hezekiah removed idolatry and remained faithful to God's commands. Despite evil and threats from the Assyrian King, God delivered Judah because of Hezekiah's obedience.

Scripture says:

Acts 5:29 (NKJV): *But Peter and the other apostles answered and said "We ought to obey God rather than men."*

Ask yourself: What do you need to be delivered from? Even in situations that seem insignificant, God sees and values our obedience. Just as John the Baptist baptized Jesus, even though he knew Jesus was sinless we must remain faithful and obedient even when we don't understand or face criticism. We trust that God keeps His promises and fulfills His will. Even after Jesus ascended, the Apostles, continued to spread the gospel out of obedience.

Whether we feel Jesus walking with us or not, we must continue to follow Him remaining obedient and faithful no matter the outcome. There will be times when people oppose us, and we may feel cast out or isolated as if we are to blame because many reject what God says in favor of worldly beliefs. Reflect on the apostles: despite criticism and opposition, they remained steadfast. If they had given up, who knows what might have happened or where we would be today?

9

2

Understanding God's Love and Purpose

God, in His boundless love, guides us daily through His Holy Spirit. When we are obedient we see His guidance and strength, just as He did with the apostles. We must remain bold in our faith, choosing to stay with Him rather than stray away. Rejection of His word leads to inevitable downfall. We must remain humble, seek Him, and strive to please Him. He provides instructions and equips us, but how we respond is our choice.

Proverbs teach us the benefits of obedience, reminding us that wisdom is a direct result of fearing the Lord. Following His instructions preserves us from evil and maintains our connection with Him. Ask yourself: Do you want to lose your connection with God? We all know the consequences of losing that connection every time.

Consider Adam and Eve, who broke their connection with God through disobedience and made excuses to downplay their actions. Reflect on your life: How do you live now and how, can you strengthen your connection with God? I guarantee that your home, surroundings, and life will be more peaceful, filled with joy only God can provide, and infused with hope that comes from a strong connection and obedience. I know I want that what about you?

Scripture says:

Isaiah 1:19-20(NKJV): *if you are willing and obedient you shall eat the good of the land but if you refuse and rebel you shall be devoured by the sword for the mouth of the Lord has spoken.*

Wow, that alone sounds scary to me.

Scripture says:

Luke 11:28(NKJV): *But He said, More than that, blessed are those who hear the word of God and keep it.*

I don't know about you, but when I read these two scriptures I find myself saying, "Thank you, Father, for all that You do and for all You have brought me through." I hope my life reflects Your goodness and I am pleasing You daily. I want to do my best to keep Your commands and remain obedient to You, in all things.

Another thought that comes to mind is...

Scripture says:

Jeremiah 7:23 (NKJV): *But this is what I commanded them saying, Obey My voice, and I will be your God, and you shall be My people and walk in all the ways that I have commanded you that it may be well with you.*

We must be doers of the Word, not just hearers; otherwise, we deceive ourselves. God reminds us that His will shall be done, not ours! Jesus humbled Himself by being obedient to the point of death, even death on a cross, and He never wavered. He remains the greatest example of obedience to God and gave us a clear path. He removed every barrier standing in our way.

Reflect on what might be holding you back. Are there barriers you didn't realize, were there until you began growing in God's Word? We all have faced them at one time or another, but as we are more obedient, seek Him more earnestly, and allow His truth to transform us, those walls crumble. This is where true repentance enters a change of mind and heart. It's an essential condition of salvation, driven by the goodness of God, His divine love, and His desire for sinners to be saved.

The consequences of sin and the demands of the Gospel are tied to the hope of spiritual life and life in the Kingdom of Heaven. True repentance means acknowledging our sin, demonstrating genuine change, and turning away from sin with true brokenness. It involves asking God to heal and forgive us, with a resolve not to return to old ways but to stay far from them. It's feeling sorrow for past wrongs and passionately pursuing godliness, removing sinful habits from our lives one day at a time. As we do this, we are drawn closer to God, growing in Him more and more each day.

Scripture says:

Matthew 4:17 (NKJV): *From the time Jesus began to preach and to say, Repent for the kingdom of heaven is at hand.*

3

The Power of Full Surrender

He has been warning us and continues to do so every day. When we truly seek Him, we can hear His words and recognize His ways. Are you listening to His voice, His call to you, those gentle whispers He brings to your heart daily? We must learn to listen and spend time with Him each day.

I know it's not always easy; it can be painful. The road is narrow, and few will find it. But if you're still reading this, it means you want to be the change. You don't want to remain stuck, going in circles like a hamster on a wheel. You desire to break every chain and stronghold, to be free from the grip of this world. And I am so proud of you! I am genuinely excited for you, to see God's love unfold and witness the steps that will help you grow in your walk with Him.

In this book, you will find scripture, but you will also find testimony, guidance, and love shared from one follower of Christ to another to help you see things in a new light. I know some people may not always understand certain words or their meanings, but I hope that by the time you finish reading, it will help to edify God's Word and illuminate the steps we must take to, fully surrender to Him. This journey is an everyday walk, not just something we do, from time to time.

The battle between good and evil, living in this world with all its challenges, and the sacrifices we must make daily can feel overwhelming. That's why we take it one step at a time, one day at a time. I promise you, it is a road worth taking to experience the love of Christ and live eternally with Him. What else could we ever need? Truly, nothing. For He will provide all we need, beyond anything we could ask or imagine, and He always provides abundantly.

Can you envision having more than enough? More than enough love, anointing, miracles, and wonders feeling so fulfilled that you no longer hunger or thirst? As you grow in Him, you will begin to see clearly and find yourself saying, "That's what it means," or "Now I see." When we surrender, completely, body, mind, and soul, we receive much more in return, and that blessing overflows.

Scripture says:

Matthew 21:32 (NKJV): *For John came to you in the way of righteousness, and you did not believe him, but the tax collectors and harlots believed him and when you saw it, you did not afterward relent and believe him.*

Jesus shows us countless reasons to believe He reveals Himself in many ways, providing signs, guidance, and moments that strengthen our faith. He gives us all we need to trust in Him.

Scripture says:

Luke 17:3-4 (NKJV): *Take heed to yourselves, if your brother sins against*
you rebuke him and if he repents forgive him, And if he sins against you seven times in a day and seven times returns to you saying I repent you shall forgive him.

That's why we don't simply shut people out. God forgives us, we are called to extend forgiveness to others. If they do not repent and turn away from their old ways and sin we may need to move on for a time. However, we should remain open to reconciliation and continue to offer forgiveness when they are ready to repent and move forward.

Scripture says:

Luke 24:46-48 (NKJV): *Jesus told the disciples, He said Thus is what is written thus it is necessary for the Christ to suffer and rise from the dead on the third day and that repentance and remission of sins should be preached in His name to all nations beginning at Jerusalem and you are witness of these things.*

He warned them as He warned us in his word of what to do or not to do.

Scripture says:

Matthew 3:8 (NKJV): Therefore *bear worthy of repentance.*

Just as Jesus instructed the disciples, He calls us daily to be fruitful, to repent, and to renew ourselves. Ask Him how you, can bear more fruit; He will reveal it to you in many ways. One way is by immersing yourself in His Word and spending time with Him. Another is engaging with materials that strengthen your walk, not just living, day to day according to your understanding but striving for something greater than He has for you. As you pursue this, becoming the new you will shift from feeling like a duty to becoming a joyful habit, ultimately transforming into a way of life.

4

Walking with God Daily

God's desire for us is to spend time with him daily

Scripture says:

Isaiah 30:15 (NKJV): *For thus says the Lord God The Holy One:*
   In returning and rest you shall be shaved in quietness and confidence shall be your strength but you would not.

God is gracious to us and compassionate but, he, also is a God of justice when we follow him and wait on him we will be more blessed for our obedience to him within ourselves.

Scripture says:

Luke 5:31-32 (NKJV): *Jesus answered and said to them, those who are well have no need of a physician but those who are sick I have* *not come to call the righteous but the sinners to repentance.*

He desires for all of us to repent from sin. He understands our weaknesses and knows when we are walking with Him. Just as the sick need a doctor to, aid in their healing, we need spiritual guidance to navigate our daily struggles. Reflect on how you think, act, and speak: Is it the flesh leading you, or is it God within you, guided by the Holy Spirit? Ask yourself if there was a moment today, yesterday, or last week when you let the flesh lead instead of following God. We must ask ourselves these questions daily, ensuring we do not lose sight of Him and get caught up in selfish ways.

Scripture says:

Acts 3:18-19 (NKJV): *But those things which God is how God foretold by the mouth or all the prophets saying that Christ would suffer, he has thus fulfilled Repent therefore, and be converted that your sins may be blotted out, so that times of refreshing may come from the presence of the Lord.*

When we come to him and leave everything behind that's exactly what we do and he receives us wholeheartedly.

Scripture says:

Acts 5:31 (NKJV): Him *God has exalted to his right hand to be as prince and savior to give repentance to Israel and forgive of sins.*

He exalts us from what we were and makes us clean with a new spirit within.

Scripture says:

Acts 20:21 (NKJV): *Testifying to Jews and also to Greeks repentance toward God and faith toward our Lord Jesus Christ.*

Paul spoke to both, Jews and Greeks trying to get them to change and help their walk.

Scripture says:

Romans 2:4 (NKJV): *Or do you despise the riches of His goodness, forbearance, and long-suffering, not knowing that the goodness of God leads you to repentance?*

God is an all-knowing God and, will repay everyone for how they lived their lives or did the works for him.

Scripture says:

Acts 11:18 (NKJV): *When they heard these things, they became silent and they glorified God, saying, Then God has also granted to the Gentiles repentance to life.*

Scripture says:

Jeremiah 31:19 (NKJV): Surely, after *my turning I repented, and after I was instructed I struck myself on the thigh I was ashamed yes, even humiliated because I bore the the reproach of my youth.*

God reveals our sins to us and instills a conviction that can be painful, making us feel the hurt we have caused Him or sensing His disappointment. These moments of realization are when we begin to experience true change within ourselves, driven by a deep desire not to let our Father down.

Scripture says:

Revelation 3:3 (NKJV): *Remember, therefore, how you have received and heard hold fast, and repent therefore if you will not watch I will come upon you as a thief and you will not know at what hour I will come upon you.*

God can allow you to be here or not just as simple as that what is his will, is his will!

5

Navigating Life's Challenges with Faith

Scripture says:

Revelation 2:5 (NKJV): *Remember therefore from where you have fallen! Repent and do the first works or else I will come to you quickly and remove your lampstand from its place unless you repent.*

The light you carry will dim, your spirit may feel lost, and your thoughts will become aligned with the world rather than with Him, risking the loss of your soul and your place with Him. That's why repentance is crucial to move forward not backward, and not to dwell on the past. Instead, focus on how far you've come and the growth you've achieved. It hasn't been an easy journey, but it is worth every step.

Scripture says:

Romans 2:5 (NKJV): *But in accordance with your hardness and your impenitent heart, you are treasuring up for yourself wrath in* *the day of wrath and revelation of the righteousness judgment of God.*

He brings all things to light, revealing truth to us and others when we abide in Him and allow Him to grow within us, one step at a time. This daily seeking of Him, the joy we experience when He speaks, and the desire to know Him more are like a child running to their parent's warm embrace that connection becomes everything, and nothing else matters. Nothing else can move or sustain us except our Father. The more we seek Him, the more we see how He magnifies everything for His glory.

Scripture says:

2 Corinthians 7:9-10 (NKJV): *Now I rejoice not that you were made sorry, but that your sorrow leads to repentance, for you were made sorry in a godly manner that you might suffer loss for us in nothing, For godly sorrow produces repentance leading to salvation not to be regretted but the sorrow of the world produces death.*

I would much rather have repentance than death, right? What about You?

Scripture says:

1 John 1:9 (NKJV): *If we confess our sins he is faithful and just to* *forgive us our sins and cleanse us from all unrighteousness.*

See repentance in all scripture shows it is not optional if we want to have a relationship with God, that is the first step in coming to faith in Jesus Christ.

Scripture says:

Acts 2:38 (NKJV): Then *Peter said to them, Repent and let every one of you be baptized in the name of Jesus Christ for the remission of sins and you shall receive the gift of the Holy Spirit.*

True repentance is rooted in faith in the Lord Jesus Christ; there is no other path. It involves a profound change of the heart, not merely a change in actions. It is a modern miracle when a human heart transforms. As Jesus told Nicodemus, "Except a man be born again, he cannot see the Kingdom of God." This rebirth makes us new creatures, and without it, we cannot inherit the Kingdom of God. those who embrace true repentance, the promise is sure: you, can be cleansed, despair can be lifted, and the sweet peace of forgiveness will flow into your life.

When we invite Him into our hearts, change begins not just within our hearts, but in every aspect of who we are. Godly sorrow, a gift of the Spirit, is a profound realization that our actions have offended our Father. He commands us to repent, assuring us through Scripture that the old is gone and a new

24

life begins. We are forgiven and transformed. It must start somewhere why not with you? He promises blessings for those who keep His commands.

God works from the inside out whereas the world operates from the outside inward. The world can lift people from the slums but Christ removes the slums from within people enabling them to rise above their circumstances.

The world attempts to mold people by altering their environment and shaping their behavior, Christ transforms individuals from within enabling them to change the world one person at a time. The relationship between repentance and faith is central to the gospel. We must first have faith in the Lord Jesus Christ.

People often ask why faith must precede repentance. To understand this, we must grasp the significance of the anointed sacrifice of our Heavenly Father. No flesh can dwell in God's presence without the intervention of His mercy and grace. The Holy Messiah laid down His life in the flesh, through faith, we receive the power of the Spirit. This resurrection power enables us to rise from the dead, with Christ being the first to rise.

6

Transformation Through the Word

Scripture says:

Romans 3:23 (NKJV): *Paul says "For all have sinned and fall short of the glory of God.*

Even the just and upright cannot save themselves solely through their own merits. Without our sinless, perfect Father who willingly sacrificed Himself, there would be no remission of sins. True repentance involves more than merely reforming behavior. While many people demonstrate significant willpower and self-discipline to overcome bad habits and weaknesses of the flesh, they may not acknowledge our Heavenly Father and may even reject Him. Positive changes in behavior alone do not constitute true repentance.

Faith in the Lord Jesus Christ is the foundation upon which sincere and meaningful repentance must be built. To genuinely turn away from sin, we must first look to Him, the Author of our salvation. As the Church, we grow spiritually when we are reborn in Him. This mighty change, brought about only through faith in Jesus Christ and by the Spirit, transforms us. The old ways are left behind through the blood of Christ, and our lives are cleansed and led by the Spirit.

With this transformation, there is no longer a disposition to return to old ways. You become, in reality, a new person, a new creation with a changed heart. Are you changed? Repentance to God means feeling sorrow for actions that displease Him and turning away from them, feeling the conviction of the Holy Spirit.

Scripture says:

Revelation 3:20 (NKJV): *Behold I stand at the door and knock, if anyone hears my voice and opens the door, I will come into him, and will dine with him and he with me.*

He doesn't merely say, "I stand at the door and wait for you to knock." Instead, He is, actively calling us, inviting us to open our hearts and let Him in. He takes our hurts and weaknesses and transforms them into strength and joy. When we embrace humility, it demonstrates that His grace is truly sufficient.

He reveals His love to us time and again we only need to seek Him to see it and to be part of what He is doing in and through us. He is our source of power and strength. All His promises are fulfilled when we remain faithful, and Scripture guides us in how to live, showing us how many promises have been fulfilled. He provides light in this dark world. Those who tremble under the Lord's power will be made strong and will bear fruits of praise and wisdom.

Satan may try to make you believe that God is displeased with you and will not hear your prayers, aiming to deceive and discourage us. The power of sin is formidable, but we need a strength greater than ourselves to overcome it. Our Heavenly Father helps us flee from sin, we must turn to Him, confessing, repenting, and seeking His help daily. By humbling ourselves and inviting His Holy Spirit to overwhelm us, we will find the power to change our lives.

We must not lose hope. Becoming Christlike is a lifelong pursuit, requiring dramatic growth and change.

Paul on the road to Damascus and Enos praying deep into the night are powerful examples of transformation, even in moments of despair. Yet, we must recognize that while these examples are real and transforming, many people find the process of repentance challenging and instead adapt to worldly ways.

We may gradually come to realize that we are building a life that reflects God's character a life of quiet goodness, service, and commitment. Like the Lamanites who were, baptized with fire and the Holy Spirit, we can approach God with a broken and contrite spirit. Through faith, full surrender, and repentance, the fire of the Holy Spirit takes over, changing us fundamentally.

We must never lose hope, as it is the anchor for our souls. Satan seeks to cast us adrift by sowing discouragement and undermining our surrender. However, God is always pleased with our efforts, no matter how small they seem. He values our daily striving to become more like Him and is pleased with our continual efforts to grow in faith.

Although the road to perfection may seem long, we must not give up or lose hope. For those who are willing to pay the price required for true repentance, the promise is certain: you can be cleansed, your despair can be lifted, and the sweet peace of forgiveness will flow into your life.

Scripture says:

Isaiah 1:18 (NKJV): *come now and let us reason together says the Lord, through your sins, are like scarlet, they shall be as white as snow though they are red like crimson, they shall be as wool.*

He transforms us from what we were into something new, blessing our obedience through our faith. The Lord spoke with clarity when He said, "Behold, he who has repented of his sins is forgiven, and I, the Lord, remember them no more."

We must remember that the past is just that the past. If we dwell on it, we risk losing sight of the future and becoming trapped in old losses, decisions, and circumstances. While we can learn from our past experiences, we cannot be consumed by thoughts of what might have been or the mistakes we made wondering, "Why did I do that?" Yes, we've all been there.

Yet, even through our missteps, we can thrive in the present and the future by growing through it all, giving everything to

God, and moving forward. The gospel is the Lord's plan for our happiness, and repentance is designed to bring us joy. True repentance is based on and flows from faith in the Lord Jesus Christ there is no other way. It involves a change of heart, not just a behavior change. When we experience Godly sorrow for our sins, this is what it means to have a broken heart and a contrite spirit.

God's gifts are sufficient to help us overcome every sin and weakness if we turn to Him for help. Repentance isn't always about dramatic change; often, it is a step-by-step, steady, and constant movement toward Godliness. When we follow this path, we qualify to be more than just members of record in the church of our Heavenly Father. The Lord has promised, "Whoever is of my church and endures to the end, he will I establish upon my rock, and the gates of hell shall not prevail against them."

That is the promise I long for to enter His kingdom and make Him proud daily. We must remain faithful and thank Him for each day we receive! Let the peace that, comes from Christ rule in our hearts, for we are called to live in peace as members of His body. That peace begins with our connection to Him and trusting, in all He has for us, confessing every sin directly to God.

Repentance may be painful and embarrassing because it brings us face-to-face with our shame, but Godly repentance is not about dwelling in shame. Instead, it is a redemptive step away from sin and a commitment to not returning to it.

God uses His disciples to help weed out what is earthly within us our pride, fears, idolatry, and assumptions so that we might see our sin, confess it, and repent. Through His mercy, offered by Jesus Christ, we are changed one day at a time. This journey of transformation is often challenging, but every step we take is worth it to our Heavenly Father. Remember, God does not forgive unrepentant sinners; true repentance requires a sincere heart and a genuine effort to change. When we submit to God with sincerity, we prove it by following Him and striving to be the change.

We must pay attention to what God wants for us; His ways are far better than ours. Our choices, actions, and attitudes should reflect this understanding. When we inspire others to become better versions of themselves, with our Father at the center of it all we achieve true success. This isn't just about fleeting moments of change but about committing to a lifetime of growth and transformation.

7

Building a closer Relationship with God

As we come to know our Heavenly Father, we will also recognize His Spirit not only in ourselves but in others. We must learn to listen to His voice, see what He sees in us, and align ourselves with His purposes. Doing what He says, rather than what we think is best, keeps us on the right path. If we rely only on our understanding, we risk heading in the wrong direction, satisfying only our flesh for a fleeting moment, not our spirit.

What we do today can change the course of tomorrow for better or for worse. Just as flowers need water to grow, we all need the living water that Christ provides. When we seek Him earnestly, we grow closer to Him and experience true fulfillment. You know that, right?

This reflection is a beautiful reminder of the importance of nurturing our spiritual lives, just as we would care for a delicate flower. Our souls, like flowers, need consistent care and attention to flourish. When we allow our spiritual needs to go unmet, we can find ourselves in a state of drought feeling dry, disconnected, and lifeless But the good news is, just like a wilted flower responds to water and sunlight, our spirits can be revived with the right nourishment.

It's important to ask ourselves regularly: What does our soul need to thrive? Is it thriving and vibrant, or is it withering in need of, renewal? Just as we would with a flower, we must provide our spirit with the living water of God's word, the light of His presence, and the nurturing care of prayer and meditation.

Even small steps, like reading a verse of scripture spending time in prayer, or taking a walk, to marvel at God's creation can make a significant difference. As we consistently seek Him, we begin to see His hand in every aspect of our lives. The more we align our lives with His will and express gratitude for His blessings, the more we feel His peace and joy filling our hearts.

Let this be an encouragement to tend to your soul daily, to give it the love, attention, and nourishment it needs to grow and bloom into something beautiful. In doing so, you'll find, yourself growing closer to God and seeing His presence in all things.

whether you're a new believer or a seasoned follower of Christ wonder if God is truly listening. We may find ourselves asking, "Does God see what I'm going through? Does He notice my heartache, hear my prayers, or understand my struggles?" The comforting truth is that He does. God sees every tear, hears every whisper, and knows every unspoken word of your heart.

He is always present, always listening, and always caring. Sometimes, it may feel like He is distant, but often it is because we have allowed the noise of life to drown out His voice. We might feel disconnected because we've neglected to nurture our relationship with Him. Abiding with God requires spending time in His presence, soaking in His word, and resting in His peace.

Remember, God has the power to calm every storm. He quiets the waves that threaten to overwhelm us and brings stillness to the chaos of our lives. When the winds of hardship blow fiercely, He is there to clear the skies and shine His light upon us, reminding us of His constant presence through the beauty of His creation like the promises found in rainbows after the rain.

So, let us thank Him daily, not just for the times when everything is calm, but also for the times He carries us through the storms. Thank Him for never forgetting us, always caring, and being our steadfast anchor in every situation big or small, expected or unexpected. No matter what comes our way, He is with us guiding loving us, and working all things together for our good.

Scripture says:

Isaiah 41:10 (NKJV): *Fear not for I am with you be not dismayed for I am your God, I will strengthen you, yes I will help you with My righteous right hand.*

He is always with us in every situation, his hand is in it all, everything we ask, seek, and feel the love He has for us is so beautiful, He tells us.

Scripture says:

Deuteronomy 31:6 (NKJV): *Be strong and of good courage do not fear nor be afraid of them for the Lord your God, He is the one who goes with you, He will not leave you nor forsake you.*

When you feel alone, remember His promise: He is always there, even when you can't feel Him. In moments of doubt and struggle don't wrestle with your thoughts alone, for our battle is not just against flesh and blood, but against the spiritual forces of evil that seek to deceive and destroy us.

Hold fast to the truth of who leads us God, our loving Father. He is the One who takes every thought captive, aligning it with His purpose. Don't let the enemy disrupt or destroy the beautiful work that God is doing in you. Remember, He has begun a good work in, you and is faithful to complete it.

Sometimes, the hardest thing to do is to be still. Yet it is in the stillness that we come to know His presence most profoundly in the quiet we recognize His hand at work in our lives see His will unfolding, and feel His love encompassing us. in being still that we begin to see the bigger picture He is painting, a masterpiece of grace, mercy, and hope.

Trust Him in the stillness. Lean on Him in the uncertainty. Allow Him to finish the work He has begun in you, and you will witness His faithfulness in ways beyond what you could have even imagined.

Many times, we face things that seem too overwhelming to

handle. Yet, we must remember that with God, all things are possible. What may seem monumental to us is but a small matter to Him. Sometimes, the things that appear big to us shrink in His presence, and the things we see as small can become significant when viewed through His eyes. It all comes down to perspective.

Think of it like taking a picture: from a distance, things appear small, but as you zoom in, they grow larger and clearer. The same happens when you go to the eye doctor, looking through different lenses to find the right focus. What was once blurry becomes sharp. In life, many things appear massive and overwhelming because we are too close and too focused on the details. But when we allow God to shift our perspective we often find that what seemed so big is quite small in His hands.

God grants us discernment to see the truth in all things when we seek Him and stay in His presence. He helps us recognize what truly matters and what doesn't. By asking for His guidance daily, He opens our eyes to the things that are worth focusing on and helps us release those that aren't.

He equips us with everything we need, even when we, feel unprepared or confused. He teaches us to see through His lens of wisdom and spiritual understanding clearing away the blurry vision that the world gives us. When we align our sight with Him we begin to see clearly, understanding that He is in control and that nothing is too big or too small for Him to handle.

Seek His guidance, lean into His understanding, and trust that He will help you see things as they are. His vision will bring clarity, peace, and the assurance that He is with you always.

Indeed, no one truly knows the things of God except the Spirit of God, who sees all and understands all. We are reminded to reflect and ask ourselves: Am I truly nourishing and feeding my spirit with what comes from God? Am I following His ways, or am I giving in to the desires of my flesh, satisfying only worldly cravings or self-centered needs?

These are deep and necessary questions because as humans it's easy to get caught up in fulfilling our desires, mistaking them for God's will. Take a moment to let that truth sink in. Meditate on it, and ask God to reveal the areas where you may need to realign your actions and intentions with His will.

Remember, He goes with us in every step. He doesn't leave us to figure it out alone. When we seek Him, He is faithful to guide us, to help us discern between the spirit and the flesh, and to lead us into a deeper relationship with Him. Let this be a daily reflection, a moment-to-moment decision, to walk in His ways and not our own.

He is there, always present, always ready to help us grow and strengthen our spirits.

You've captured a powerful and essential aspect of the Christian faith the transformative process of being "born again" through both, water and the Spirit. This rebirth signifies a profound change in one's heart and life, rooted deeply in faith in Jesus Christ.

Jesus' teaching about being born again, as recorded in John 3:3-5, highlights that this transformation is crucial for entering the Kingdom of God. It's not merely about physical baptism, but about a genuine, spiritual renewal a new birth from above, facilitated by the Holy Spirit.

This concept of rebirth is more than a one-time event; it's an ongoing journey of becoming more like Christ. It involves:

1. Faith in Jesus: Believing that He is the Son of God and accepting Him as Lord and Savior.
2. Spiritual Renewal: Allowing the Holy Spirit to transform and guide us, aligning our lives with God's will.
3. Living Out the Faith: Embodying the principles and teachings of Jesus, as shown in His life and ministry.

Jesus' example of being baptized and receiving the Spirit underscores the importance of following His steps. His baptism was not for repentance but to fulfill righteousness and set an example for us. By aligning our lives with His teachings and the guidance of the Holy Spirit, we embark on a path of continual spiritual growth and transformation.

Reflect on these truths, and ask yourself:
  - Am I living a life that reflects this new birth?
  - How can I deepen my relationship with God and allow His Spirit to guide me fully?
  -In what way, can I live out my faith in daily actions and decisions?

As you seek to live a life filled with God's presence, remember that He is always with you, guiding, supporting, and transforming you from within.

You've touched on a crucial aspect of following Christ total surrender and commitment. Jesus made it clear that true discipleship involves not just acknowledging Him but fully embracing His teachings and instructions, including the significance of baptism. This act of obedience symbolizes our identification with Christ's death, burial, and resurrection, and it marks the beginning of a new life in Him.

Here are some reflective questions You can ask yourself:

1. Am I All In?: Are you fully committed to following Christ, or are there areas where you're holding back? True faith requires total surrender of your heart, mind, and will.
2. Am I Letting Go of the Past?: Are there past mistakes or hurts that you're holding onto, preventing you from fully embracing the new life Christ offers? Christ's forgiveness, means you are no longer bound by your past.
3. Inner vs. Outer Focus: Are you focusing on external appearances or societal expectations or nurturing a deep, personal relationship with God? The change that matters most is the transformation of the heart.
4. Returning to Your First Love: Are you returning to your first love Christ daily, or are you allowing distractions and the busyness of life to pull you away? Renewing your relationship with Christ involves consistent devotion and love.

5. Full Surrender: Are you giving God a portion of your life or fully surrendering everything to Him? Genuine faith requires an all-or-nothing commitment.

6. Trusting God's Plan: Do you trust that God has a plan for your life, even when things are difficult or don't make sense? Believing in His plan involves faith that He will use all circumstances for your good and His glory.

Even when life is chaotic and heartbreaking, God remains a constant source of strength and hope. Your faith journey is personal and ongoing. It involves daily decisions to align your actions with your beliefs, trusting that God is working, in and through you, even when the results are not immediately visible.

By trusting in God's promises and embracing His process, you can navigate life's challenges with His grace and guidance. Your willingness to fully engage in this journey reflects a deep commitment to a life transformed by His love and power.

You've captured the essence of God's unwavering presence and love beautifully. Even when we feel overwhelmed or lost, God is always there, breathing life and strength into us. His love remains constant, regardless of our past or our struggles. Trusting in His plan allows us to see His will unfold in his, perfect timing. When we surrender fully to Him, He restores what's broken and brings comfort and peace to our lives. True faith is about being all in, not just giving part of ourselves but dedicating our entire being to Him. It's important to reflect on whether our faith is built on a firm foundation, knowing that God's love and commitment are unchanging.

You've beautifully articulated the unwavering presence of God in our lives, especially during our most challenging moments. Your words remind us that God's love and support are constant, even when we may feel lost or overwhelmed.

Here are some thoughts:

1. God's Presence in Difficult Times: It's reassuring to remember that even in our darkest moments, when we feel like sinking, God is there, breathing life into us and giving us strength His presence is a beacon of hope and resilience.

2. God's Unchanging Love: No matter where we've been or what we've done, God's love remains unchanging His commitment to us is steadfast and His belief in our potential never falters.

3. Trusting in God's Plan: Even when we don't have all the answers, we can trust that God's wisdom and plan are perfect. Surrendering fully to Him allows us to see His will and promises unfold in His time, which is always best.

4. Restoration and Comfort: God's ability to restore our brokenness and bring comfort and peace is a testament to His love. When we invite Him into every part of our lives, He works to mend what's broken and guide us toward healing.

5. Being All In True Faith requires full commitment. It's not about giving God part of ourselves but dedicating our entire being to Him. This complete surrender allows us to experience His transforming powerfully.

6. Firm Foundation of Faith: Reflect on whether your faith is consistent and built on a firm foundation. A strong

relationship with God is not dependent on circumstances but grounded in His unchanging nature and promises.

In the journey of faith, remember that God's love is not contingent on our actions or worthiness but is a constant, all-encompassing force. Trust in His plan, stay committed to Him, and know He is always there, guiding, supporting, and loving you through every moment.

Since Christ has become the life-giving Spirit, we can now receive God's life into our spirits through regeneration as a re-birth. To receive this life, we must first repent to God and believe in the Lord Jesus Christ. We need to invite Him into our hearts with openness and honesty. After asking Him in and repenting of our sins, we surrender everything to Him, laying it at His feet. We then get baptized in the Holy Spirit, marking our rebirth as a profound transformation within our souls and desires. This transformation leads us to be baptized in water, starting a new life of salvation following God's plan.

8

Freedom Through Christ

However, the journey does not end there. We must align ourselves with Christ, follow Him, join life groups, nourish our spiritual growth, and mature in our new birth. when we Fellowship, with other believers it enriches our walk with Christ and helps us experience all the blessings our Father has in His presence. It is crucial not to doubt your salvation or question your experience of God. God's Word is steadfast and true, regardless of what others say or think. Every word in the Bible is God-inspired, and God-breathed, and we also have an internal witness from the Spirit confirming our salvation.

Even when we may not feel it, our inner spirit will affirm that we are children of God. Trust in your salvation and let the new you, guided by the Spirit, walk in the light of this new life.

Scripture says:

1 John 3:14 (NKJV): *We know that we have passed from death to life because we love the brethren He who does not love his brother abides in death.*

He also promises that whoever believes Jesus Christ has risen from the dead and confesses with their mouth that Jesus is Lord will be saved. This includes calling upon the name of the Lord, as Scripture assures us that such a person shall be saved. In today's world, this love is impartial, embracing both those who are alike and those who are different. This is the true oneness and harmony that the world seeks, and it becomes ours when we receive Christ.

God chooses us and loves us, even in our sins. He is a loving and righteous God, with righteousness and judgment as the foundation of His throne. Reflect on your life right now are you living in a way you are proud of? Is there room for improvement? We can always grow, no matter where we are in our faith journey. We should never be stagnant in our faith. God desires us to grow closer to Him, every day and not limit what He can do. He is an omnipotent God who wants us to prosper daily.

One way to grow is through gaining knowledge of His Word, which offers new perspectives and deeper understanding. Even when we hit a plateau in our spiritual growth, we should push deeper, as there is always room for more learning and growing. Knowledge helps us align with Christ and keeps us accountable for our steps, including when we stray from His path. These small convictions or decisions are God's way of guiding us back to Him, even when the path may seem dark. He provides a beacon to guide us, helping us see the way even from afar.

When we trust Him, He reveals many miracles and wonders. However, we must be careful not to lose sight of Him or become distracted by the things of this world. Stay focused on Him, and He will continue to lead and bless you.

You might face challenging situations and wonder why you're going through them. Remember, as children of God, we are honored to be called and used by Him. You are qualified not because of your merits but because God has chosen you. Each one of us is called by God to fulfill His purposes. It is a blessing to be entrusted with His plans. Don't shy away from your calling, even if it seems beyond your understanding.

Are you actively seeking God? If not, what's holding you back? When you surrender to God, the process may not always come with immediate, dramatic revelations. Spending time with God and seeking His guidance should be a priority. It's important, not only to read the Bible or follow routines but to genuinely desire to connect with God.

While gaining knowledge from the Bible is crucial, it's equally important to prioritize your relationship with God. Your time with Him should be about wanting to grow closer, not just fulfilling an obligation. Your walk with God is unique, and growth happens at many different rates for everyone, Be patient and persistent in seeking Him and allow His presence to guide you through the journey.

Here are reflection notes:

1. God's Call and Qualification:

- You might face challenging situations and wonder why you're going through them. Remember, as children of God, we are honored to be called and used by Him. You are qualified not because of your merits, but because God has chosen you.

2. Understanding Our Call:

- We are all called by God to fulfill His purposes. It's a blessing to be entrusted with His plans. Don't shy away from your calling, even if it seems beyond your understanding.

3. Seeking God:

- Are you actively seeking God? If not, what's holding you back? When you surrender to God, the process may not always be with an immediate dramatic revelation.

4. Spending Time with God:

- Spending time with God and seeking His guidance should be a priority. It's important to read the Bible or follow routines but we must genuinely desire to connect with God.

5. Balancing Knowledge and Relationship:

- While gaining knowledge from the Bible is crucial, it's equally important to prioritize your relationship with God. Your time with Him should be about wanting to grow closer, not just fulfilling an obligation.

6. Patience and Growth:

- Your walk with God is unique, and growth happens, at different rates for everyone. Be patient and persistent in seeking Him and allow His presence to guide you through this journey.

Living a life, with God isn't just about setting aside time each day; it should become a natural, integral part of who we are a habit that defines us. Just like babies start by crawling and then learn to walk, eventually running and jumping, our spiritual growth follows a similar path. Initially, we might stumble and fall, but with, persistence and faith, we grow stronger and more capable.

Our strength and growth depend on the effort we invest. Things don't come to us effortlessly, especially if they aren't aligned with God's will. In God's Word, He reveals many truths and directions. It's up to us to embrace them fully, saying, "I'm ready, God. I surrender everything to You. I trust You completely and will follow Your guidance every day."

This surrender is not just a one-time event but a daily commitment. Even when things are challenging or unclear, trusting God allows us to move beyond obstacles and hardships. The journey might feel like a roller coaster but with God's guidance, we can overcome anything meant to destroy us.

If you're wondering where to start or how to grow remember that spiritual growth can be challenging initially, but it becomes second nature over time. For, new believers or those seeking to deepen their faith, the Gospel of Mark is a good place to begin. It introduces Jesus and His teachings, helping you engage with Scripture and understand what it means to follow Him. Ecclesiastes offers insight into human existence and the emptiness of life apart from God.

Ultimately, knowledge and wisdom are valuable, but having a personal relationship with God is essential. This relationship allows us to understand and live according to His intended purposes.

Genesis provides a profound foundation for understanding God's original design and intentions for creation. It's incredible how it sets the stage for everything that follows, showing not just the origins of the world, but also the blueprint for how God desires us to live. The Gospel of John on the other hand, really brings to life the purpose of Christ's coming and how His life serves as a model for us. Together these books give us a comprehensive view of God's plan from creation to redemption.

The Book of Luke is a profound and detailed account of Jesus' life shedding light on the human condition and the depth of His sac-rifice. It's a powerful testament to the cost of discipleship and the fulfillment of God's purpose through Jesus' resurrection.

Reflecting on the sacrifice of Jesus truly underscores the depth of His love and commitment. He endured the unimaginable, knowing the suffering and rejection He would face, all for our freedom and salvation. This sacrifice wasn't just a moment of bravery it was a profound act of love and obedience, carried out without hesitation or doubt.

In Colossians, we see how we are called to grow in Christ and embrace our complete identity in Him. We are rooted in Him, alive, free, and hidden in His grace. This understanding helps us grasp the magnitude of what it means to live, in His promises and be part of His church.

The concept of everlasting life is a remarkable promise, One that encapsulates the hope and future we have in Christ. It is a life where all promises are kept, not just some. Sometimes, the waiting period can be challenging, but it is in these moments that our faith is tested and strengthened. It reveals our trust in God's timing and His plans for us.

Every task no matter how small is a step toward fulfilling God's purpose for us. Trusting in His timing and being patient as we wait for His promises to unfold is part of the journey of faith. It's a journey that leads to growth, fulfillment, and ultimately, a deeper relationship with God.

It's amazing to consider how our lives are shaped by our choices and how deeply our faith impacts our daily lives. In 1 Peter, we learn about the significance of having a new identity in Christ and how it equips us to endure trials and tribulations. By submitting to God and living by His Spirit, we can overcome the fleshly desires that often distract us from our true needs.

The Scriptures are rich with guidance on how to grow in our faith

Books like Romans and Ephesians provide practical insights into how we can live out our belief in Christ daily and support others in their journey of faith for new followers some passages might seem challenging but as we seek God's guidance and wisdom, understanding deepens, and His teachings become clearer.

The transformative power of God's word is not just theoretical but practical. As we immerse ourselves in Scripture and follow His lead, our actions, speech, and overall way of life reflect the new understanding He imparts to us. This transformation is not just about changing our behavior but about a profound shift in our inner selves.

Our growth in faith often comes with moments of reflection and realization, recognizing how far we've come and how much we've been changed. Even seasoned followers may find themselves grappling with new insights, but with God's help, we gain clarity and continue to evolve in our spiritual journey. Embracing this process allows us to live out The new identity we have in Christ, demonstrating His love and grace in every aspect of our lives.

Deuteronomy highlights the crucial choice between life and death, urging us to choose life in everything we do to glorify God and embrace the prosperity He offers. In contrast, the Book of Psalms provides solace in difficult times, guiding us to praise God through every season, and reminding us that His worthiness to be praised transcends all circumstances.

Isaiah offers a deeper understanding of Christ's identity and the suffering in the Old Testament, frequently quoted in the

New Testament, illuminating the story of salvation. Micah emphasizes the necessity of repentance for sin, underscoring that salvation requires turning away from the old ways and seeking forgiveness.

Acts illustrate the gospel as defined in Romans and Mark, emphasizing that there is no correct way to begin our journey with God. Instead, God will guide us through our relationship with Him and the Holy Spirit. As we dwell in His presence and seek His guidance, we gain revelation and a deeper understanding of His word.

All scripture is God-breathed, offering us guidance on living a life of love and purpose as outlined in His divine letters.

The Word of God! Whether you begin with a shorter book like Psalms or Proverbs or dive into longer texts, remember that every step is a move in the right direction. Many people find Psalms or Proverbs accessible due to their wisdom and clarity but start with what resonates with you. choose a Bible translation that you understand and can read easily.

Your journey doesn't need to be rushed; it's not about how quickly you read or how many pages you cover in one sitting. What truly matters is your relationship with God and your commitment to growing closer to Him each day.

Consider starting by highlighting the verses that speak to you or writing them down. As you progress, use methods that suit your learning style, whether note-taking, memorization, or another approach. The key is to find what helps you best remember and internalize Scripture, even if it takes time.

Pray before, during, and after your reading. Let God speak to your heart and guide your understanding over time. This practice will transform your thinking and life Through this intimacy with God, you will discover your purpose and identity in Him. You'll find peace, comfort, and forgiveness beyond what anyone else can offer. Even in moments when you feel unworthy, His love remains steadfast. This deep connection ignites the divine fire within you and strengthens your walk with Him.

9

Finding Purpose and Direction

Embrace this journey with openness and patience, and let your relationship with your Heavenly Father grow deeper each day.

Time is incredibly precious, and spending it wisely, especially with Christ, ensures we experience everlasting life with Him. Genesis introduces us to the origins of creation and flood as well as, the promise made to Abraham. Books like 1 John, 2 Timothy, Ephesians, 1 Corinthians, and Colossians all emphasize belief in God the Father, Jesus Christ the Son, and the Holy Spirit. The Ten Commandments in Exodus and Deuteronomy provide moral guidance, while the Gospels of Matthew and Luke recount the birth of Jesus, and the accounts in John, Mark, and Luke detail His death, resurrection, and ascension. They also speak of Christ's second coming, the day of judgment, and salvation for the faithful.

John, 2 Corinthians, and Ephesians address the fall of man, showing that all have sinned. Romans elaborates on salvation and the necessity of fully surrendering to God's will. To understand and receive these blessings, we must read His word and seek to follow His guidance step by step.

It is crucial to remember where our power comes from, as highlighted in 2 Corinthians, which describes how we become a new creation through Christ. Regardless of which part of the Bible we read, the essence lies, in time with God a daily priority. Don't let the light within you fade by neglecting your spiritual nourishment. Stay connected and keep the flame of faith alive by feeding your soul with His word.

We need to make our relationship with God one of our highest priorities, like breathing. It's not just a duty but a necessity for living fully. Without Him, we would falter, but with Him, all things become possible. Never forget that in all your learning and growth, His love is the force that makes everything possible.

Some passages in the Bible can indeed feel overwhelming or confusing, but God is there to transform our uncertainties into understanding. As we grow in our faith, we grow through challenges and discover potential we never knew we had. His Spirit shines within us and guides us. All we need to do is let Him lead. If you, find yourself unsure or confused, ask Him for clarity He will provide, and often more than you expect.

It's a leap of faith to trust where He leads us and requires a willingness to, fully surrender As Gentiles, we need to recognize that not everything in the Bible was originally written for us, but God wants us to grasp all He has for us. Just as understanding a Jewish Bible or their customs might be challenging due to cultural differences, so can understanding parts of Scripture that seem foreign or difficult to us.

A relationship with Christ means following Him, not just adhering to religious traditions or interpretations. The Old Testament and New Testament are not separate entities but a unified whole, with the New Testament building upon the Old. The Bible is God-breathed and meant to be understood in context. Some passages may initially seem confusing, but as you grow, God will grant you a deeper understanding of every meaning in His word. Keep seeking Him, He will illuminate your path and make sense of the scriptures.

James provides foundational wisdom for our walk with the Lord, emphasizing the power of our words and the essence of true religion. Through Scripture, we uncover profound lessons and interpretations, but our Father is always there to guide us when we seek His wisdom. He illuminates our path, helping us see things with greater clarity.

God is unchanging yesterday, today, and forever more He reassures us not to worry or fear about our needs; He provides for us in His perfect timing. When we place Him first in our lives, everything falls into place. Let Him dwell in your heart, mind, body, and soul, cultivating within you the incorruptible beauty of a gentle and quiet spirit, which is precious in His sight.

Jesus declared, "I am the way, the truth, and the life." No one comes to the Father except through Him. His sacrifice was perfect and complete, and His way is the only path to salvation.

Let us remember and hold fast to all He has taught us, trusting His way is the way to eternal life.

Scripture says:

1 John 1:5-9 (NKJV): *This is the message which we have heard from him and declare to you, that God is light and in him is no darkness at all. If we say that we have fellowship with him and walk in darkness we lie and do not practice the truth, but if we walk in the light and we have fellowship with one another and the blood of Jesus Christ his son cleanses us from all sin, if we say we have no sin we deceive ourselves and the truth is not in us if we confess our sins he is faithful and just to forgive us our sins and to cleanse us from all unrighteousness.*

If we accept the testimony of men, surely the testimony of God is greater. it is God who has testified about His Son. We are called to walk in the light of Christ, following Him daily and dying to our flesh and the darkness of this world. being living sacrifices for our Heavenly Father, we are cleansed of all sin through His blood, receiving forgiveness and mercy because of His great love for us.

We must love and forgive ourselves as He has forgiven us. Our salvation is not based on sight or feelings but on faith and surrender. Though human and imperfect, we are called to turn from our sins and move forward, carrying our cross and seeking more of Him. In doing so, He grants us discernment to see what we might otherwise miss and conviction to turn away from temptation. Each time we falter, let us run to Him, seeking forgiveness and expressing gratitude for all He provides.

Scripture says:

1 Corinthians 15:3-4 (NKJV): *For I delivered to you first of all that which I also received that Christ died for our sins according to the scriptures and that he was buried and that he rose again on the third day according to the scriptures.*

We must remember that Jesus died for us to live, removing all sin and bestowing us righteousness. As new creations, the old has passed away and the new has come. We are called to manifest His righteousness, in our lives through faith belief, surrender, repentance, and His grace. Through these, we are saved and experience a rebirth.

Scripture says:

Ephesians 2:8-10 (NKJV): *For by grace you have been saved through faith and that not of yourselves it is the gift of God not of works lest anyone should boast for we are his workmanship created in Christ Jesus for good works which God prepared beforehand that we should walk in them.*

Even though we are not worthy of his love he forgave and gave it anyway his love is so great that he wanted us to have all good things.

Scripture says:

James 2:24 (NKJV): *You see then that a man is justified by works and not by faith only.*

James teaches us that genuine faith in Jesus will naturally, produce a transformation in our lives making the evidence of our faith shine through effortlessly. Paul further guides us to examine ourselves to ensure we live by faith rather than by our fleshly desires. He emphasizes our salvation is not earned by our works but is a gift of the Lord's grace. Even before the world began, God prepared good works for His children to carry out.

Scripture says:

Hebrews 10:24 (NKJV): *And let us consider one another in order to stir up love and good works.*

We are saved not by our works but by them. Jesus keeps His promises, and the Holy Spirit dwells within us, giving us the hope of Christ's return and guiding us to glorify Him. This is why we die to our flesh and live in the Spirit. "Since we live in the Spirit, let us walk in the Spirit." We must be guided by the Spirit daily, feeling His presence and control in our lives as we grow in our relationship with Him. Following His lead means remaining pure in spirit, not conforming to this world, and fighting the good fight by giving it all to Him. We soak in every word and verse, aligning them in our hearts, and allowing the light within us to shine outward.

When storms come or seasons feel dark, we will not be shaken because the light within us shines brighter than any darkness. The temptations of this world will not move us; we remain planted on a firm foundation with Him, rooted from within. We strive to please our Heavenly Father daily, moving from sinful desires that grieve our souls. God gives us the strength, power, and authority to stand against the schemes of the enemy, Even when spiritual attacks come, we know who fights for us. We ask God for strength praying boldly for these attacks to flee, and they will because the enemy knows we are steadfast and unshaken.

We seek God's peace, which only He can bring, in times of hurt, grief, strained relationships, loss, trials, and uncertain circumstances. By preparing our hearts and aligning our thoughts with His, we remain strong and find the peace and joy needed to navigate life's challenges. When we stay focused on Him, we won't sink. Our minds fixed on Him will discover perfect peace, grace, love, mercy, and hope gifts that nothing else can provide.

God does not want us to live with worry or fear. Instead, He invites us to surrender our burdens to Him, allowing Him to carry them every time. When our thoughts and choices are aligned with His, we focus on what truly matters. His love for us is deeper than we can ever comprehend, yet He reveals it to us through Scripture, where He also teaches us how to love. Paul reminds us that while faith and hope are vital love is even greater. It's His love that we should seek daily a love that is righteous and rooted in truth.

Godly love guides us to live with a clear understanding of His will for us It includes forgiveness, nurturing strong relationships, being obedient, and sharing His love, grace, and forgiveness with others. When we die to ourselves we must pick up our cross and follow Him daily. He promised we would face suffering, but He also equips us with everything we need to endure. No matter the cost, we follow Him. Whatever we lose for His sake, He will return with greater blessings. We are called to be unashamed of Him and His Word, sharing it with all we encounter As we walk with Him, we experience His Spirit's joy and happiness, and His light guides us.

In turn, we become a light for others, drawing them closer to Him away from the chaos and darkness of this world one step at a time Consider how you can be a light Even if you're beginning your journey, God can use you. No one is ever too far gone to be used by Him. It doesn't matter if you're new to this walk or have been on it for years. It's not about how long you have been walking; it's about the depth of your relationship and your willingness to be used by Him.

Ask yourself, "Am I willing to be used by God? How can I be a light?" Is your soul filled with His love, mind, body, and spirit? I understand this might feel overwhelming, especially if you're starting. Your thoughts might feel scattered, and the path ahead may seem unclear. But ask yourself, "If not now, then when? Why not now?" Let your desire and passion for God take the lead.

I know it isn't easy; every day can feel like an uphill battle. But when you reach the top when you overcome and grow, imagine the joy that day will bring. God has already overcome this world and equipped you to do the same. Don't stay stuck; don't turn back only move forward. I understand that when you've been hurt or broken, the unknown can feel frightening. I've been there more than once, feeling more broken each time. Yet, it is in those moments that God is closest to you.

It wasn't easy to get through all that I faced, but reaching the top of the mountain I never knew existed has been worth every step. Remember, if the path were easy, everyone would take it. But the journey, with all its challenges, leads to a place of unimaginable joy and peace.

Many people turn to the things of this world because it feels easier and more familiar it's what everyone else seems to do. But God! He gives us the power to break free from all those strongholds, to rise above, and to break those cycles and generational curses. He empowers us to do more than we ever thought possible. So, ask yourself again: Why not now?

And if you're already walking with Him, going through challenges but feeling unworthy or broken, remember that God will help you through it all when you surrender it to Him. Life will hit us with many things some big, some small. But as we grow in Christ, we keep moving forward, breaking free, and finding our breakthrough. Remember your worth, and remember your value. The only person who can stop you is you. You have the power to either step into your calling, purpose, and growth or hold yourself back.

Often, we blame others for what they did, what they're doing, or how they made us feel. But it's not about them or their walk it's about you and your walk. Your journey will not look the same as theirs, and it's your choice whether to go all in or not. You hold the keys to a life worth living or a life of destruction. You have the choice to either keep revisiting the broken pieces of your life or leave them where they are.

We need to reach the stage in life where we leave those broken pieces where they lie. Don't try to repair what God hasn't called you to fix. If anything is worth restoring, God will lead you back to it; otherwise, keep moving and growing. When you do, you will begin to see your breakthrough. We've all been broken at one time or another some more than others. But God! He rebuilds us from the inside out. He changes us and helps us see through His eyes.

Those pieces that we thought mattered, we release them to Him. If they are meant to be in our lives, they will remain; if not, He will remove them far from us. We may see ourselves as broken, unworthy, not enough, confused, or hurt. But God shows us otherwise. He shows us how beautiful we are, reveals our calling and purpose, and equips us with everything we need. He gathers all our broken pieces to make us whole again, every single time. He is always there.

He places us in situations we never expected, in places we have never heard of but where we were always meant to be. He aligns everything to fall into place at just the right time His perfect time. He repaired all that hurt us confused us and stood against us. He removes from our lives what doesn't belong, setting us free from past hurt, pain, guilt, fear, or anything that holds us back. Through His grace, we experience a rebirth and a refining from within.

We begin to see the light of His love and understand all that He wants for us. The more we surrender to Him, the more we see that everything that once broke us is now molding us into who we were always meant to be. The light within us begins to shine, and we see the beauty of the life that God has been preparing for us all along.

Take a deep breath in and out as many times as you need. As you do feel His peace flow over you, calming your heart and mind. Take a moment to thank God for His Spirit, love, mercy, and grace. Allow the Holy Spirit to guide you today. Soak in His love, and remember that His will, not ours, will be done. Trust that He knows what is best for you, beyond your desires or plans. How incredible it is to have a Father who loves us deeply and who desires far more for us than we could ever imagine. Once we decide to move forward, to let go of what holds us back, we begin to grow. We don't have to stay stuck in the past or dwell on what we've done wrong. Remember, we have been washed clean of all our mistakes, forgiven, and given a new beginning. We are called to run from our past, not return to it. Trust that God is molding you into who you are meant to be, step by step.

God knows exactly what He is doing. We may not always understand His ways and it may not always make sense to us, but we need to trust Him. Everything you have been through has a purpose. God sees the bigger picture and He is orchestrating, everything for your good and His glory. He doesn't want us to look back at our failures; He wants us to focus on our future. Don't dwell on who you were; look ahead to who you are becoming. Remember who you have in your heart, who fights for you, who goes before you, beside and behind you. He will never leave you nor forsake you. Keep fighting the good fight of faith! Don't look back; hold on just a little longer. Your breakthrough is closer than you think. Let go and let God.

Be who He has made you to be. Our lives can only go as far as we allow Him to take us. If we're not willing to surrender completely, we limit what He can do in and through us. He is not meant to be confined to a surface level; He wants to go deep within us. Don't hold back; God is more magnificent than you can imagine. Allow His presence to fill you, bringing peace, joy, and purpose with every breath you take. Embrace all He has for you, and remember how deeply loved you are. Don't stay stuck in the past or settle for less when there is so much more He wants to show you.

Are you willing to go all in? Are you ready to see what He has in store for you? You are forgiven, and set free from your past sins, hurts, fears, and anxieties. All of that has been washed away. Do you trust God? If your answer is yes, then trust in His plan and let Him lead you into the future He has prepared for you. Even to those mountain tops no matter how steep they are he will not let you fall, trust God always.

Scripture says:

Romans 10:8 (NKJV): But what does it say? *The word is near you, in your mouth, and in your heart. (which is the word of faith which we preach)*

This is the word of faith, we are called to preach, but what are you doing with it? Where is your faith rooted? Where is your spirit anchored? Remember, He is always with us; He never leaves or forsakes us! The Lord is by your side in every moment, through every trial and triumph.

10

The Joy of Fellowship and Community

Do not lose sight of what He is trying to accomplish in your life. Ask yourself: Have you truly surrendered to our loving Father? Are you living as a genuine, breathing sacrifice, dying to your flesh daily and allowing His Spirit to lead you? Stay connected to Him keep your heart in tune with His love, and let His presence guide your every step.

Let your faith grow stronger, your spirit soar higher, and your trust in Him deepens. Hold on to His promises, knowing that He is faithful to complete the good work He has begun in you. Don't let the distractions of this world pull you away from His path. Instead, draw nearer to Him, and let your light shine as a testimony of His love, grace, and mercy. Stay anchored in His truth, and let His peace and joy fill your heart.

Scripture says:

Mark 12:30 (NKJV): *And you shall love the Lord your God with all your heart and with all your soul and with all your mind and with all your strength this is the first commandment. when we are passionate and feel full of purpose it drives us.*

Just like when we read stories and the characters leap from the pages, awakening our deepest desires, we too long for passion in our own lives a, passion that fills us with purpose. We were created to be captivated by such passion; God designed us with a desire, for something more that satisfies the longing within us according to His divine plan.

The greatest story of passion is the one where Jesus gave Himself completely for us, for all our sins. His profound love and sacrifice were driven by a passion, to lead us all to salvation and freedom, to impact eternity by bringing more souls into His Kingdom, and to set people free from the darkness of this world.

We are made to live with passion, but too often the church loses people because they feel there isn't an opportunity to live as passionately as God intends. Instead of growing in Christ, they return to worldly pursuits. Yet, as the Book of Mark reminds us, "Anything is possible if a person believes." God desires all of us every hidden part, every scar, every bruise, and every secret we hold deep within. He wants us to align with Him, to find that passion that moves us and compels us to surrender all to Him.

He calls us to come to Him day and night, not just within the walls of a building or during gatherings, but also in our quiet moments and secret places. It is in this intimate time with Him that our passion grows, preparing us to embark on the journeys

He has planned, to step into the unknown, away from a life of simply getting by. He wants us to experience the peace of Heaven and to know that this world is only temporary, while what He offers is eternal.

Every hurt, every storm, every struggle is worth it for the sake of His presence. God's story is timeless a narrative woven through the ages to prepare us for an encounter with Him that has an everlasting impact. Yes, it may cost us everything, but everything is nothing compared to what He gives.

Some people will not understand, and until they have the eyes to see with full surrender, they might call us crazy or think we've lost our minds. And that's okay because in a way, we have. We have lost all of ourselves; what once was is now gone. And that's where we begin to see His beauty: in the unknowing yet knowing we are in good hands, guided by the Holy Spirit toward His direction, to the destinations He has chosen for us.

Many followers of Christ will not reach the places they are meant to be and will miss out on a life filled with the full encounter of God because they lose focus. They get caught up in the familiar patterns and distractions of this world, forgetting the cost He paid for us and what we must be willing to do for Him. They stray from the promises He has set before them, and without pursuing Him wholeheartedly, they will not live a passionate life or fulfill all that He intended for them.

To live a life that is truly full and satisfying, we cannot cater to the desires of the flesh or remain lukewarm. If we do, we drift far from God and risk missing the mark. Yet, we have a chance right now to pick up our cross and live a life that matters, a life with true meaning. When we choose this path, we will find ourselves strengthened every single day. Not waiting on a certain day or feeling instead we take that leap of faith with Our loving Father that starts with the first step!

Scripture says:

Philippians 4:13 (NKJV): *I can do, all things through Christ who gives me strength.*

And He truly will. The more you seek, the more you ask, He will re-ignite that fire and passion you once had. He will give you that drive that brings you closer to Him every day. Remember, He's waiting on us, not the other way around. The more we trust, the more we will see.

Open your heart to all He has for you and the overflow will come a love so powerful that you won't, be able to contain it. It will break out and break free. Let your "yes" be a firm, unwavering "yes." Maintain that unbreakable connection and be in unity with your loving Father. Strengthen your relationship with Him so it does not slip away because of lost focus or waning passion. Trust in all He has for you, and keep pursuing Him daily!

Scripture says:

Jeremiah 17:7 (NKJV): *Blessed is the man who trusts in the Lord* *and whose hope is in the Lord.*

Let God be the change within you! Don't surrender to the lies of the enemy or the world. Allow Him to reignite your passion and that fire waiting to blaze forth. Make it your commitment to only walk in paths that align with His will. If you sense that God isn't in it then, choose to let it go.

Coming to Christ and transforming your life is not an easy task. Each step closer to God often invites the enemy to try and steal your joy and redirect your path. The enemy will make you think it's acceptable to delay your commitment or to justify small sins but remember sin is sin whether big or small the act of sinning and allowing it to take root in your life is what separates you from God.

God permits temptation to test us, but He does not bring it; the enemy does. Don't entertain sin seek God in all things, and the enemy will flee. It's crucial to recognize, that not everything that seems good is from God. The enemy knows you well and can disguise his intentions. Stay grounded in God's Spirit and the enemy will have no foothold.

It's challenging, and you may face situations or people who seem to offer what you need, but remember: the enemy often masquerades as something good. Trust in the Spirit's discernment and remain close to God. Even when you fail and we all do don't let it deter you. Let go of what's holding you back, and move forward.

Everyone experiences temptation, even Jesus did. Stand firm, set yourself apart, and show the enemy he has no place in you. You possess the power and authority to overcome temptation. Understand this, believe it, and walk confidently in it. Embrace the daily walk with God, knowing it will be challenging, but will also be fulfilling Through storms, trials, and temptations, we grow stronger and more aligned with His will.

God may not always act in ways we expect. Sometimes, He withholds things to protect you, strengthen you, or test your response and faith. Ask yourself, "Do I trust God fully? Do I see Him in my circumstances?" Even when it's hard to see Him, He is present. Trust in His word and promises.

If you're reading this, thank you for your commitment. Congratulations on your desire for more! Remember, each day is a step toward growth and deeper trust in God. It's His way, not ours, and we must adhere to that. Ask Him for guidance, doors to be opened, a changed heart and mind, and a deeper relationship. Commit to these changes actively. Faith without works is dead. Surrender to Him, trust, and be obedient. As you do, your faith will grow stronger, and everything will fall into place as you follow Him on a firm foundation. I know this is a lot and some things we must do are repetitive but it's also being consistent and obedient in our faith something that we become stronger every time we grow and how we were last year will not be the person we are next year, trust God's guidance he does not fail!

The enemy will come, but you will not be shaken. This doesn't mean ignoring his presence; instead, prepare for those personal struggles, those deep-seated triggers known only to you and God. Surrender these to Him and embrace His protection by

71

putting on the full armor of God. Be strong in the Lord and His mighty power.

The battle is unavoidable, and though the enemy often appears invisible, remember GOD is omnipresent, He performs miracles daily and is eternal. Through our relationship with Jesus Christ, we are seated with Him in heavenly places. Our struggle isn't against flesh and blood but against spiritual forces.

The real enemy is not the people who hurt us or the circumstances that challenge us; it's the spiritual attacks behind them. The visible mental, emotional, physical, and financial issues are connected to unseen spiritual realities. The enemy wants you to focus on the visible to subtly shift your direction away from God. Though he may be invisible, he's real and persistent, bringing spiritual warfare into our daily lives. This results in chaos, anger, unforgiveness, pride, fear, and more.

But God comes to our rescue, every time we remain faithful and grounded in Him that's why He gave us His Word our guide and road map to equip us against everything contrary to Him. We must engage with all of Scripture, not just select passages that resonate with us. The entirety of His Word offers understanding and guidance, which the Holy Spirit illuminates as we seek Him.

As we draw near to God our understanding of Scripture deepens revealing new insights and meanings. This growth aligns us more closely with Him and His guidance. Don't overestimate the impact of Satan or prioritize the seen over the unseen. The enemy hides himself to make us forget his presence and to build schemes that lead us astray from our destiny in Christ. Utilize, the spiritual resources God provides and stay vigilant against the distractions and conspiracies designed to detour your path.

Those spiritual forces are scheming to divert us from all God intends for our lives. We possess the strength to stand firm against the enemy's manipulations, which seek to distort God's truth and lead us into sin, breaking our connection with Christ. In our moments of vulnerability, the enemy preys on us, attempting to keep us trapped and powerless. The temptations we face during our weakest moments are all part of his plan to prevent us from experiencing the abundant life God has prepared for us.

Remember, the battle begins in the heavenly realms, which is why we must equip ourselves with His Word. Standing firm in the battle, knowing who fights with us and for us, ensures that we, will not falter. We are seated in heavenly places with our Father how beautiful is that? God has granted us victory; it is finished, and we are victorious in Christ. When you gave your life to Christ, you transitioned to a position of victory, bringing that experience to earth. The enemy cannot destroy you, though he will try through sin, temptation, and others to divert you from God It's your flesh that must decide to resist or yield, and he uses intimidation to make his lies seem true, aiming to sever your connection with the life-giving Source.

We must not let the enemy lead us astray. Remember who cares for us and is within us. As children of God, when we remain focused on our connection with our Father, the bonds that try to hold us will, not only be burned away but strengthened. God is always with us, and our faith in His Word grows stronger each day We will shine brighter, overflowing with His love.

73

11

Living Set Apart for God

God sees and hears all, loving us despite our imperfections. He knows our thoughts and sins before we act upon them. Our actions reveal whether we are bearing the fruits of the Spirit or succumbing to fleshly desires. Sometimes, we need to retreat into solitude, immersing ourselves in His Word and seeking His quiet presence to discern His guidance. These moments of solitude are essential, but if we don't seize them, we might miss seeing God's work in our lives. He is with you wherever you go; you are never truly alone. God's eyes are upon you, and He gives you the ability to perceive His presence when you abide in Him.

It's not just about reading His Word or writing but feeling His embrace, especially in times of fear or doubt. God wants to exchange your turmoil and chaos for His peace and goodness. When you start to recognize Him in your daily life, your spirit will resonate with His presence, and you'll crave more of His touch. This is when miracles and wonders unfold because you're open to surrendering everything, leaving behind shame, guilt,

74

doubt, and excuses. Jesus has paid the price for all, declaring us worthy, free, and forgiven without condemnation. He knows our struggles and intercedes for, us having given us the Holy Spirit to lift us from deep waters and draw us closer to His heart.

The Joy of You may wonder how to strengthen yourself. The truth is, it is God who provides the strength you need. As you grow and overcome past burdens, don the full armor of God to protect your heart. People may view you differently and try to hinder your journey, but keep moving forward! Keep seeking, Keep loving, and do not stop, no matter how challenging the walk may be. You are not alone in this fight. This reality alone is a testament to His love.

As you embark on this journey of complete surrender remember to hold nothing back. The people who leave your life were never meant to be there. The ones who remain will be shown to you by God and your new self will experience love and connection more deeply. You are a new creation a new, person who understands your identity in Christ. Let this identity guide you. Even though starting anew is difficult, trust that each day, one step at a time will bring you closer to the strength and transformation God has promised.

We've all had to start over at some point, some of us, more than once. And that's okay. Each time you start anew, you're better equipped. You understand the meaning of full surrender and what it means to be a living sacrifice for Christ. Even if you haven't fully grasped it yet trust that you will. Trust in God, and everything will fall into place just as it's meant to. Remember seeing isn't always believing we must live by faith, not by sight and each day we should move forward, leaving behind the old self as a testimony of how God has delivered us.

When you give up and lose the will to fight for peace, your passion, and belief in yourself, others, and God can become clouded. Without hope, freedom seems out of reach, and you may find yourself ensnared by addictions and losing interest in prayer. Distancing yourself from God is exactly what the enemy wants. He aims to make you doubt God's ability, to strip away your hope and connection to God, pulling you into valleys of despair where you feel stuck and overwhelmed. But remember, in those moments, there's a powerful truth: BUT GOD!

He calls you to embrace your Heavenly Father's gifts, to knock and have doors opened, to seek and find. He offers strength and equips us with His power to stand firm and overcome. Victory is ours already! We must believe in receiving this victory. Belief in God's power and staying faithful through prayer, focus, and obedience, builds our foundation. We must be prepared for everyday battles, guarding ourselves against spiritual attacks.

God works in you daily, encouraging you and renewing your fight. He wants you to take your faith seriously, to stand strong against the enemy. Your faith, resolve, and willingness to fight determine your victory. The enemy and our flesh will attack, but we must remain vigilant and intentional. Distractions and weaknesses must not deter us. Our faith must be activated, recognizing that struggles are temporary and God is with us in every trial.

Even in the fires of life, we are shielded by our faith. We can hold our heads high, knowing that when the lights go out, the true light, God, shines brightest. He is a God of restoration and renewal, giving abundantly when we fully trust and surrender to Him. Just like a flashlight needs batteries to shine, we need to go to the source, of light to power our lives. Though it may seem difficult, remember that God is with us every step of the way. He helps us navigate each struggle, and His presence is constant, even when unseen.

This journey of surrender, laying everything at His feet and trusting His ways, leads to seeing the bigger picture. We begin to understand God's greater plan and experience His goodness, even in moments of difficulty. I am proud of you! Yes, you! Because you, are willing to surrender beyond your understanding to the one who gave you life and cares for you in every way.

Heaven is celebrating as more people like you, choose to fully surrender to God, trusting Him over their desires, and casting aside concerns about worldly opinions. This journey is uniquely yours, a personal walk with God that others cannot accompany you. When you face our Maker, it will be a one-on-one encounter, a deeply personal moment of unity and conversation. Can you imagine that day?

We look forward to living with God in a new world, a place where sorrow, hurt, and fear are no more a place completely unlike this earth. What a beautiful day that will be! But until then, we must prepare, trust, and keep God with us in all that we, do each day, growing closer to Him and His ways. So today, spend time in His presence; I guarantee you will not regret it. Be expectant for the, more you seek Him, the more you will find. When you think you've reached the limit of what you know, He will reveal even more, bringing new feelings and deeper understanding.

Scripture is God-breathed and alive, revealing new meanings each time we read it. The words themselves do not change, but we do. As we grow, He prepares us more for the destination He has in store and the purposes we are meant to fulfill on this earth. It's a process of being molded and equipped, growing stronger in faith and wisdom. We can never learn too much; the wisdom, we gain helps us follow His path rather than the world's.

By becoming addicted to God and His Word, we let go of worldly addictions. Our foundation is firm because we know it is built on the rock of Christ. When storms come, we remain standing, supported by battles our Father fights on our behalf the battles we may not even know about. We are strengthened by our full surrender and trust in His will over our own, loving as He loves us, becoming living sacrifices as Jesus was for us.

In this daily walk, we strive to live as God intended, moving away from lukewarm faith and the ways of the world. We no longer follow man but God alone. It is through this surrender that we see His love, mercy, and hope more clearly, and begin to envision our future with a renewed, spiritual light. As we fully surrender to the Lord, He reveals the path we are meant to walk.

God, the Creator of all things, chose us to live a holy life one that is blameless and free from sin. Holiness, defined as being

78

separate or set apart just as God is, is a call that remains steadfast. This divine purity of holiness comes from within and reflects God's purity.

Paul, in Ephesians, reveals our identity in Christ. God has chosen us to be His children, embracing His wisdom, power, and love. Our response should be one of obedience, living in a manner that honors Him. We are called to be set apart, to live blameless lives, not by our strength but through His presence within us.

We are God's treasured possessions, a holy nation chosen by Him. How incredible is it to be, chosen by God! What a profound testament to our worth in Him. As a loving Father, He desires to see our light shine brightly in this dark world. We are to become beacons through His Spirit, embodying our identity in Christ as living sacrifices that are holy and pleasing to Him.

Even though we are called to live in ways that honor God, we are still human and prone to fall. The key is not to remain in our failures but to move forward, seeking His forgiveness. Confession and repentance bring us back to our forgiving Father who is faithful and just. When we pursue Him and acknowledge His Spirit within us, we begin to experience the empowerment that comes from growing closer to Him.

The more we grow in our faith the more the Holy Spirit can guide us, leading us to live, righteous lives. This journey of, living in holiness is not always easy it can be challenging for both new and seasoned believers. Yet, it is a journey worth undertaking it brings us closer to our Father and fulfills His divine purpose for us. Are you ready for this walk down this road less traveled?

Reflect on your life today and consider how far you have come. What has God done for you? What challenges has He helped you overcome, or obstacles has He removed from your path? Take a moment to thank Him for your life, for the lessons learned, for the breath in your lungs, and for His unending love. Then, move from that place of gratitude into praise. Engage in prayer, worship, or any connection that brings you closer to Him. I guarantee that this practice will make your journey easier.

God will guide you to the right scriptures, revealing truths that will resonate deeply in due time. There are no limits to what our Father can do, and His ways are unlike anything this world can offer. Whether your walk with Him is just beginning, progressing slowly, or has been ongoing for years, what matters is His presence. As long as God is with us, He continues, to guide and reveal new things.

Don't feel discouraged if you think you've reached a plateau or are unsure where to go from here The answer is always to turn to God seeking, reaching, loving, and growing in ways you never imagined. Whether it took a year or ten, what matters most is your relationship with Christ and your commitment to follow Him daily.

Our Father delights in our return to our first love, revealing the true essence of love beyond physical and emotional, but deeply spiritual it's, a profound realization to understand your identity in Christ and to recognize the worthiness of His boundless love. You are a child of the Most High!

Thank You, Lord, for Your love and the gift of coming to You, wherever we are and however we are. Thank You for enabling us to fully surrender to Your Spirit, embracing Your guidance, and equipping us for what lies ahead.

People often ask, "What does it take to surrender? What should I do or say?" My answer is always to seek God with your whole heart. Surrender is not just about a prayer of repentance or asking for the Holy Spirit it's about being a living sacrifice to the One who gave His life for us. It's about serving without expecting to be served following wherever He leads, and preparing your heart to fully receive His blessings. It's about growing in faith, standing firm on the foundation of His love, and living each day with the confidence that His will is being fulfilled. Embrace the journey with Him, one day at a time, living out the life He has given you.

Many say it's not our works that earn us a favor but our faith. However, remember, faith without works is dead! We must act to fulfill God's will and purpose for our lives. We can't simply wait and expect things to change or be provided without taking action. Our works are the evidence of our faith they show how we follow God's will and how our speech, actions, and love reflect His guidance. This transformation isn't a one-time event it's a continuous journey. Every day we should strive to deepen our relationship with God, regardless of the chaos around us.

Storms will come, as they always do, but we have the assurance of victory through Christ. He walks with us through fire and darkness, even when it feels like everything is collapsing. Even if we can't see Him because we are too focused on worldly concerns, He is there. But God arrives like a fresh wind, guiding us every step of the way.

Start today! Don't overthink how or what to do. Just begin. Seek our Father with a full surrender and repent, turn away from sin, and walk closely with Him. Dive into Scripture, engage in worship, and converse with Him. The more you invest in this relationship, the more you will see your new life unfolding.

12

Preparing for Spiritual Battle

If you've been walking with Him but feel disconnected, it's time to reconnect. Ask Him to cleanse your heart, renew your spirit, and open your eyes. Seek His Word again with fresh eyes and ask for discernment to understand it anew request His embrace and guidance on how to love and be loved as He does.

God promises that if we ask, we will receive; if we seek, we will find; if we knock, the door will be opened. Are you ready to reignite your spiritual fire? Start today, but commit to keeping it lit both inwardly and outwardly. Go to your quiet place with Him, listen intently, and follow His voice. He will guide you, one day at a time, in His perfect timing.

Consider this when you deposit money into a bank you expect it to be there by a certain time and you trust that it will be available as expected despite occasional delays or fees. Similarly, God expects us to trust Him with our spiritual deposits his promises are reliable, though sometimes they may seem delayed or come, with challenges. Trust that what He provides is greater than what might be lost. If we can trust a bank to manage our funds, we should trust our Creator, who made all things to fulfill His promises.

Remember, the goal isn't material wealth but serving God wholeheartedly, regardless of what we receive or don't receive. Our faith calls us to live in service, embracing His will above all else.

When we ask for something be it a spouse, a job, or any desire it might not come in the form we envisioned or hoped for. The relationship may be challenging and not what we initially wanted. But remember, things worth having rarely come easily; they require effort and dedication. When God ordains something in our lives, He will make a way. We must trust that His plan is for our greater good.

In relationships true love involves working through difficulties to fulfill God's purpose. It's about allowing His will to be done, even if it means enduring hardships. Sometimes, God is preparing us or our future partners, working on our hearts before we receive our blessings. Similarly, a job we longed for might turn into a trial, revealing that it wasn't meant for us. Sometimes, God shows us that something we thought we wanted was never truly for us.

But God! What He has planned for us surpasses our imagination. Yes, it still requires effort, but the outcome is far greater than anything we could have envisioned. It aligns with His perfect will which is always better than our plans. As we seek Him, we, start to understand that the process is a journey we all share. No one has an easier path; what makes it bearable is knowing who walks with us through our daily trials.

Each of us has our testimonies. We face tests, trials, and tribulations sometimes even trauma that lead us to find God in our lives. These experiences help us see His beauty and grow stronger. They prepare us to assist others in their times of need. Through every cycle of struggle and growth, God is with us, guiding, strengthening, and helping us emerge greater than before. It's easier said than done but overcoming these challenges reveals that He was with us all along.

Our lives are uniquely different, each crafted in our, distinct way for a specific purpose While our journeys may vary the ultimate goal is the same to turn to God and follow Him. Although our paths are different, they all lead to the same destination of unity in Christ.

God, in His infinite wisdom, designed each of us with intention and care, creating us in His image with meticulous detail. Every aspect of our being reflects His artistry, and despite our differences, we are all part of His grand plan. The beauty lies in how, despite our diverse experiences and journeys, we are all brought together through our shared pursuit of Him.

Scripture says:

Psalm 44:21 (NKJV): *Would not God search this out? For He knows the secrets of the heart.*

God knows exactly where our thoughts will lead us and how our lives will unfold based on the paths, we choose and our perspectives on life. When we encounter something and recognize it for what it is we know to expect. But when the unknown comes, it can be challenging.

Consider a book labeled Holy Bible you expect it to be the word of God. But if the cover were blank or labeled Love Stories, you wouldn't know what to expect from its contents. Similarly, imagine a dish like lasagna, which looks delicious. If the menu failed to list hidden ingredients like fish crab or shrimp it could be life-threatening for someone with allergies like myself.

This principle applies to life as well. Many people present things in a way that, seems appealing whether to enhance their image or to attract others. Yet, they may overlook how misleading this can be, potentially leading to dangerous outcomes. The truth, however, sets us free. When we use it to speak and bring others to Christ, it's a powerful tool. While truth may sometimes be uncomfortable or unappealing, it remains essential.

Some try to soften the truth to make it palatable, thinking it will lead more people to Christ. They believe by focusing only on love and avoiding harsh realities, they will be more effective. However, the word of God remains unchanged, and we must speak it boldly. Even if people are initially resistant we continue to share the truth and plant seeds of faith. Over time, some may become ready to hear and receive all, God has for them, despite the struggles or sacrifices involved.

True surrender comes when we accept that suffering and challenges are part of the journey just as Jesus endured for us. This is when we fully embrace our role as Christ's followers seeing with the eyes of our Father and opening ourselves to new possibilities. The walk of faith is not for the weak it's for those who are strong enough to lift others and help them find the strength God provides daily. As we stand firm, we are supported by the one who has overcome the world guiding us through both trials and triumphs in this temporary world. Our surrender is not for our benefit alone, but to honor our Father, show our love and trust, and draw closer to Him, experiencing the embrace we so deeply yearn for.

This journey of faith is not a race to be won by speed or by reaching the finish line first. Instead, it's a profound, enduring journey that sustains you, even when you feel empty. As you draw closer to God, you will be replenished by His love, becoming ever hungrier for His presence. Remember, though, that as you grow closer to Him the enemy will, intensify his attacks. He targets areas of your life such as family, relationships, health, and work. These attacks might come as, vengeance, disagreements, distractions, loss, or hurt.

Stay vigilant and expectant but also, steadfast in keeping God at the center of your life. This is how you will overcome any attack that comes your way. The enemy plays dirty and aims to wear you out, to pull you away from God, wanting you to revert to your old self. But God has washed you clean from your past and he assures us daily of His presence and strength. We have the authority to rebuke any evil that comes our way. This is why, it's crucial to stay prayed up and immersed in His Word day and night.

It's not just physical attacks you'll face, but spiritual ones as well, For new followers, this might be especially challenging, but even seasoned believers face struggles. It's okay not to understand everything this is why we turn to God for answers. He will provide what we need, when we need it, as long as we remain faithful and obedient. God will guide us every time we trust Him wholeheartedly.

When the enemy strikes, know that God, stands guard, protecting you from both, seen and unseen threats. The enemy exploits our human tendencies, passions, and weaknesses, aiming to make us vulnerable and cripple our heart, mind, and soul. He works when we are distracted or not vigilant. Without knowledge of God's Word, we are left exposed which is precisely what the enemy desires.

But as we seek to learn more and grow in our walk with Christ we begin to see the bigger picture the path God has laid out for us. Our journey may not, be clear all at once, but looking back, we see how far we have come and how God has guided us through it. Transformation happens, and the things that once tempted us or held our interest start to fade. Our new desires align with Christ and His movement in our lives.

Today, reach out for all that God offers. He is only a prayer away, an embrace away, a cry away, a conversation away, a worship away. He knows your heart and spirit. When you align with Him, you will find that the world loses its appeal. You will see it differently and realize that what matters most is our loving Father and how we can bring more to His Kingdom for His glory. Trust that your dreams of experiencing His love in profound ways can indeed become a reality.

God is capable of all things yes, all things! Sometimes, it's not just through words that He communicates with us. It's also through the beauty of visions, the creations around us, and even the gentle breeze through your hair. These are the ways He shows us how He wants us to see and experience life.

When we surrender to Him, the journey doesn't end there. We must continually seek to learn more about Him and understand the guidance He has provided us. Even when the path isn't clear, He equips us with everything we need to navigate this world and prepare for eternal life with Him. By carrying Him in our daily walks and keeping the Spirit's fire burning within us, we allow ourselves to be transformed.

There is no specific formula or predetermined method for this journey. It's not about following a ten-step process to achieve a perfect result. This is a lifelong journey of evolution and change. God doesn't seek to change us; He invites us to follow Him and, through that, become transformed.

He gave His Son so that we could have everlasting life. Our response should be to fully surrender ourselves desiring more of Him and less of ourselves. Each day, as we take steps guided by Him, we feel the Holy Spirit's presence, within. We move to a higher plane where we are no longer merely existing but truly living in alignment with His will.

As we live spirit-led lives, we prepare ourselves for what is to come, shielded by faith and set apart from the world. When you start to see things through God's perspective, understanding what truly matters, you reach those defining moments of full surrender. Have you experienced that transformative vision?

Think about your defining moment when you felt that shift, that pivotal change. How did it impact you? Was there a clear instance when you realized you needed God to take control, or are you still waiting for that moment to unfold?

Really, dig deep into your experiences. Many people face their storms and struggles, but often, it's that decisive moment when they've had enough and surrender to God that stands out. Reflect on your journey. Did you experience a transformative moment? How did it affect you? Did it lead to change for the better or the worse?

Did you feel anger or blame towards God? Were you afraid or overwhelmed? Or did it bring you a sense of sadness or, perhaps, a surprising peace?

Whether you've had a noticeable defining moment or are still awaiting one, it's important to recognize that these experiences are part of everyone's journey. They shape us, challenge us, and ultimately guide us closer to understanding God's presence and purpose in our lives. Remember, it's through these moments whatever they may be that we often find our path and deepen our connection with Him.

So, if you've experienced such a moment or if you are anticipating it know that it's a universal part of the spiritual journey. It's through these defining moments, that we are shaped, refined, and drawn nearer to the divine.

God asks us to do something and we listen every time, He asked me to go to a few people I know and ask them about their full surrender, He said to ask:

What was your defining moment in surrendering fully to Christ?

So, being obedient I did what he asked and I know so many people from all walks of life so it would not be hard to do right? Well, when God asks, it is not always that easy if you know what I mean, He gave me the people to ask, it was not just who I wanted to ask it was whose story he wanted to be heard.

I have many family, brothers, sisters, uncles, aunts, family of Christ my chosen family, and friends that have various testimonies from many different walks of life. I wanted to share a few so whether you have had that defining moment when you knew you had to give it all to God or not maybe these will help in your walk and strengthen and encourage you so you know that you are not alone God is always with you and many have been in similar situations as you or pretty close some maybe worse some not so much as yours but in every situation, God was there and they are now living testimonies for him and now guiding others to God helping others out of that darkness or hurt they once had. In all these short testimonies it was a longer process but I summed it up, to help you understand. And how their lives changed. In their own words.

Think about your defining moment. Have you had one that reshaped your life or drew you closer to God? Or perhaps you're still waiting for that pivotal experience. Dig deep and reflect on this: many of us go through our storms and struggles, and often it's in these moments of intensity that we reach out to God, desiring His control and guidance. Consider how these moments have impacted you did they bring about change for the better or the worse? Did you find yourself angry or afraid? Were you filled with sadness or unexpectedly found peace?

No matter where you stand today remember that everyone experiences these defining moments. They shape us, sometimes leaving us feeling alone or uncertain. But in these trials, God is ever-present, working in ways we might not always see or understand. For many of us, these moments are the catalysts for, transformation, leading us closer to Him.

13

Embracing Daily Renewal and Growth

I want to share a few testimonies from Christ's people who have each walked through their valleys and emerged transformed. I hope their stories might resonate with you.

These testimonies while condensed here, represent longer journeys of faith and perseverance. Each one is a reminder that no matter how dire the circumstances, God is present, guiding and sustaining us. Their experiences underscore that we are not alone in our trials God is with us, and He transforms our suffering into testimonies of His grace.

As you reflect on your journey, know that these stories are not just about what others have endured but also about the hope and strength available to all of us. Whether you're in the midst of your defining moment or looking back on it, remember that God's love and power are evident in every story, and He is ready to guide you through whatever comes next. You are not alone. God is with you, and through every storm, He is shaping you for something greater. Embrace His presence, draw strength from these testimonies, and continue to seek Him with all your heart. Your story, too, is a testament to His faithfulness.

I did not put any names but I am putting numbers so you know when a new one begins,1,2,3, etc. This is to give you an example of how God moves in mighty ways in different people's lives no matter their walk, or status, God can move anyone at any age there are no limits when it comes to God! He does not discriminate he loves us all the same even if we do not deserve it he does it to give us a chance at a new life one that is filled with the abundance he brings. Are you ready for it? hope this helps

Person number 1

My life-defining moment to surrender fully to Christ, was when I knew I could not do anything for my son and anger took in and had to fully submit to God and let him take over him and let his will be done letting him control it all, not my flesh and had peace knowing it was God's to take care of, not mine and not to react but to sit back and let him take the wheel I trusted in him to lead everything and I found my peace and calmness see you have to think if it is fully surrendering or if your holding back because that is what makes the difference from it being your flesh or Gods ways taking over you yes we are human and fall short but that's why we continue to listen to him spending that intimate time with him where he brings us the strength and gives us our peace back.

God shows us in many ways even with our children at times we

94

can not see we surrender it to him and give him all control so we do not hold back from what he has for us and we move forward to the next chapter of life he has for us with his peace, love, and blessings.

Person number 2

My defining moment to surrender to Christ fully was when I lost everything and wanted to kill myself He shook me and I told him I could not do it on my own and gave him all control and knew I had to trust him and he would give me everything I lost and more. He said, You must die to the flesh, that is when I knew I had to fully surrender and let him lead everything because he was enough, it was a Job moment for me that I trusted he would fill every void!

See when we are at a breaking point he comes in and rescues us and brings victory where we can live for him knowing he keeps every promise and what we lost is nothing compared to what we will gain in return from him his love is sufficient.

.

Person number 3

My defining moment to surrender to Christ fully was when I was tired of hurting, crying, being alone, and feeling all the emotions of what I, was feeling I almost gave up on life and I told him I could not do it alone or on my own and finally fully

surrendered it all to him and he took over me and landed on the floor faced down when I raised I was a different person and what the world brought me and his power took it I was sick and tired of being sick and tired and he says all you have to do is surrender to me and John 16 came to mind and it showed me how he was speaking to me and he showed up to lift me from myself he rescued me!

John 16:1 (NKJV): *The Word Of God Says, These things I have spoken to you that you should not be made to stumble.*

There are many ways God shows and when we look and listen to what he is speaking that is when we can see and change in a way that is not our own it's so much bigger.

Person number 4

What was your defining moment in surrendering fully to Christ?

It was when I was living in the world I knew I had to surrender My family before I lost them fully and could have lost my marriage so I asked him to show me and, he did when he told me things that were going to happen, hearing his voice and, then it happened he said it would it really opened my eyes to his love and power and, I was never the same and never went back I became changed and continue to because I let him lead now every step of my life.

God comes to us in many ways and wants to show us his love it is not to control us it's to show us a better way of living that is filled with the love, he brings and we are on the verge of losing he comes to help and protect us once we give it all to him we become that change day in and day out and are never the same.

Person number 5

What was your defining moment in surrendering fully to Christ?

I finally did when I went to prison and saw this scripture Die To Flesh, If things did not work out it was because it was not from God then a reflection I saw from a vision light of the world, light out of darkness, and it showed me to be very grateful and also thankful for what he gives and how he gave more of his light in and began to walk by the spirit daily!

God shows up no matter where we are in this world even in these dark places we never thought we would see him he comes in to shine that light so we have no more darkness only the light being led by his spirit to shine throughout the world! Sometimes it happens through visions he gives to help guide us away from this dark world so we can truly see his light! Sometimes that is the only way we can.

Person number 6

What was your defining moment to fully surrender to Christ?

It was when I found out who my father truly was and who I was looking for and what I was looking for anyone to fill the void no matter if it was a temporary fix and all the time it was only him that I needed he filled the void and filled me I was in awe and my heart finally got full see we have and will deny him but he will never deny us I was in my thirties and it is the same with certain people he gives us everything we need spiritually I became a witness of Christ and had to forgive myself and all my convictions and share my testimony to help others to come to him all the things I have done and who I was I am not the same and now the only thing I need is him!

There are many times we think people or things will fill the emptiness or hurt but it only puts a temporary band-aide on what God is doing those things do not last they feel good at the moment but God sustains us in it all and he is everlasting those are temporary and those things do not last and no longer matter or mean anything because God shows us greater and the things that truly matter not what we think does or did.

Person number 7

What was your defining moment to fully surrender to Christ?

It was when I knew I had enough and I could not do it on my own and had to let guide me and went all in no more, the old was gone I was washed clean and went from there in full surrender to God and let him use me to be that servant for him as I did that he used me in many ways and I have seen so many miracles and wonders I never thought possible but it is all for

his glory all of him no more me!

Have you ever witnessed a miracle? Even a small one? WOW GOD! He can use us to see those things or to help heal others even in our pain when we are a servant to God and fully surrender there is nothing he will withhold from us all the things we did not think were possible become possible and the things we only heard about or read about come to life before our very own eyes what an amazing God we have to give us the power, authority, and sight to be part of things we never even imagined. We are not limited to anything when God is in control he is limitless we must remember he is omnipresent and sees things before they happen just as he knows the beginning and end of our lives our thoughts, and our hearts when we align with him that power is so beautiful!

Person number 8

What was your defining moment in surrendering fully to Christ?

Mine was more of a gradual move one step at a time I noticed the more he took away from me healing from my anxiety, depression, and worry, being anxious, little by little he strengthened me and with time it changed me and I know I did not want to go back, it was only forward one day at a time gradually gaining strength and a stronger faith I never knew I could have.

WOW, GOD, he moves in many ways sometimes longer than others but he shows up and shows up daily how loved we are and how he has so much more for us when we fully surrender to him our lives change.

Scripture says:

Psalms 37:18 (NKJV): *The Lord knows the days the upright, and their inheritance shall be forever.*

Yes forever! For eternity!

Person number 9

What was your defining moment to fully surrender to Christ?

It was when I tried and tried over and over to take my own life I became reborn again and God told me your story is not ending this way, I was spiritually and emotionally done I was so done and so blind so much so I blamed God for it all and did not want to listen to him even though all I went through was my own doing. This night was so different I was at my breaking point as he lifted me off my bed he gave me the ability to see he had more for me and I knew I was done with my old ways of living my life the one of the world to living of things that were not of God and had finally changed then I fully surrendered to him not to being lukewarm or following him sometimes but it was all of me, mind, body, soul! And my life was never the same. I knew he became the change within me.

Many can not see past their hurt and feel as if they have no other choice BUT GOD! When we surrender fully to God he takes all of what we thought would break us and changes it for his good, restoring us greater than before, and all the brokenness is repaired no more hurt no more fear no more anger no more lust no more adultery no more lies no more destruction, no more additions, etc. no more of anything! God brings all joy happiness peace love greatness comfort healing restoration refining he embraces his children and strengthens them to see the beauty from ashes from within come out. What an amazing Father we have, WOW! WOW! WOW! Just think about that for, a moment we get to a breaking point we can't take anymore and, he says, yes you can! I'm not done with you and I'm going, to use you for my glory are you ready to glorify me?

Person number 10

What was your defining moment in surrendering fully to Christ?

Mine was during my divorce I decided to follow him not be under my parents' prayers, and wanted it just to be me and him, I was raised to know of him but only when I fell and I wanted to know him completely not just in my fall or hurt not just my past but knowing him in my future and loving him

was and is also part of loving myself and knowing his plans are greater than my own and are what was best for me!

We all deal with things differently but when we bring God into it the perspective changes We are never the same and we know his plans are so much greater than we can think or imagine all for his greater good for his will!

Person number 11

What was my defining moment to fully surrender to Christ?

It was when God brought me out of my addiction not just from drugs but alcoholism as well and took all I thought I needed and gave me eyes to see differently it was like waking up and my life was changed in an instant and the people as well, most were gone, most did not want God to be their guidance they wanted this world and the addiction it brought to rule them and nothing that was in my way could block what God was doing and still doing daily and little-by-little the change became me and who I was. Yes I struggled, Yes I had things in my life that came to destroy me but God helped me see the victory in it all and for once I have seen things differently. Daily he showed me more of his love how he wanted me to live my life and the difference between what I wanted and what he gave in his love I let him lead and I followed in everything and continued to live as he was holding my hand guiding me in this world to the next.

There are many people, who come to Christ at their lowest but other times God comes in and rescues them before they hit rock bottom, he does what he has to just, to reach us nothing is impossible when it comes to our Father. Our salvation is like a rock hard to move but then we see the joy of it other times tend to get upset feelings hurt, and act on things we should have left alone that is why we must stay grounded in his word, cultivating, strengthening, nourishing it daily we don't just surrender and forget and live our lives the same as we once did we become new a new creation formed in his image of our father and we confess our sin and the Lord continues to cleanse us.

1 John 1:7-9 (NKJV): The Word Of God Says, *But if we walk in the light as he is in the light we have fellowship with one another and the blood of Jesus Christ his son cleanses us from all sin.*

When we confess our sins, He is faithful and just, to forgive us and cleanse us from all unrighteousness. His blood is sufficient; it cleanses us completely, restoring our fellowship with Him. Just as David sinned, prayed, and sought God's forgiveness and was restored, we too can be made whole. When He cleanses us, the old is gone it is finished, and we have the victory!

Scripture shows us how to live and feeds our spirits with truth. It is vital to gain knowledge of these love letters and strengthen our relationship with Him. In all His truth, He desires us to store His word in our hearts, even beyond the overflow so we can experience His joy. As our hearts begin to rejoice, His word comes alive in us.

It is through soaking in the Word, seeking the light even in our darkness, that God shines His light on everything. As we pour out our hearts, crying to our Father, and seek His love, we open our spirits to connect with Him in ways that transform us from within.

It's not always about the words we speak, nor the eloquence of our prayers. Sometimes, what we say isn't even of our own making it's the Holy Spirit guiding us, connecting our hearts to the Father. The power of prayer is not in its length, big or small, but in the sincerity of our hearts reaching out to His. When we align our hearts with Him, He brings people into our lives to walk alongside us, to share in the journey, and to uplift each other in prayer.

This is one of the greatest joys of being a follower of Christ beyond even our communion with the Father. It's the blessing of fellowship, of growing together, learning from each other, and sharing life's experiences with those who love Him too. In these moments, whether in trials or triumphs, we, find ourselves praising Him with renewed spirit and deeper gratitude.

So, cherish those God places in your path. Lean into the relationships He's given you, and let the love, wisdom, and encouragement flow freely. Because in this shared journey of faith, we are strengthened not just by our relationship with God but also by, the community of believers He surrounds us with.

We have the assurance, the security, and the joy of our salvation. For this, we must praise Him for He alone is worthy of our praise for the gift of full salvation! Just as we need food and water to live or oxygen to breathe, we need our spiritual life sustained by the blood of Christ. What He accomplished on the cross did not end there He lives within us, moving through us as we navigate each day.

Though we are born into a fallen state, a reality set in motion by Adam and Eve, God offers us a way back to Him. We may carry the burdens of our humanity, but God comes alongside us to guide and help us, ensuring we do not feel alone or separated from our Father. Through His grace, He made it possible for us to live moment to moment in His presence. So when sin comes our way, we repent and turn from it, finding restoration and alignment with Him once more choosing not to return to what has been left behind.

By remaining in His presence, we find strength to move beyond our fallen ways, closer to His love and purpose for our lives.

The blood of Christ is stronger than anything Satan can bring our way. He is our defender, and through Him, we can defeat all evil. The One who loved us first with His precious blood allows us to live in God's presence every day. Remember who walks beside you His strength is always with you.

We all have a voice and the choices we make matter. Some might feel their life doesn't matter, but their friend's or family members' lives do. If you feel, that way, you're mistaken. Every life, matters, including yours. The decisions you make, have a ripple effect; they can either contribute to change or cause destruction. The more we allow His light to shine from within the more we become agents of that change starting with ourselves.

We can help transform this world, one soul at a time, one step at a time, guided by our Father. When we fully surrender, the mountains and walls in our way must move, for the One who lives within us created them and has given us the authority to overcome them. We are equipped with the same power He breathed into our lungs. Even if you feel weak, remember with God all things are possible. We must trust His timing, believe, that His way is always better, and see His purpose and love in everything.

You have a purpose! God gave His only begotten Son so you and I could have everlasting life it wasn't for nothing.

For instance, one friend faced a life-altering illness that seemed insurmountable It was in the depths of this struggle that they fully surrendered to God finding unexpected strength and peace in His presence. Another experienced a period of profound loss and grief, where doubt and anger were constant companions. Yet, through the pain, they discovered a deeper relationship with God and a newfound purpose in helping others heal.

God gives us the ability to see things no matter the trail that comes he is in the storm with us always waiting with arms wide open.

Here are a few more testimonies that might resonate and encourage you:

1. **From Darkness to Light:** One dear friend of mine battled a severe addiction for years. It felt like an endless cycle of despair and relapse. But one day, in a moment of utter hopelessness, he reached out to God with a raw and honest prayer. It wasn't an immediate fix, but over time, with God's guidance and a supportive community, he began a new path.

Today, he shares his story to help others find hope and recovery, showing that, even the darkest struggles can be transformed through faith and perseverance.

See how good God is to use our testimonies for his good.

2. **Lost and Found:** Another member of my chosen family faced a painful divorce that left her feeling isolated and unworthy. In her lowest moments, she questioned God's plan and felt abandoned. But through counseling, prayer, and a renewed focus on God's love, she found healing and a deeper understanding of her worth.

She now helps others who are going through similar experiences, offering compassion and guidance, and her life is a testament to the power of God's restoration.

3. **A Journey Through Illness:** A beloved uncle was diagnosed with a life-threatening illness and faced a difficult treatment process. He wrestled with fear and anger, questioning why this

was happening. Yet, in his suffering, he experienced a profound sense of God's presence and peace.

His faith was strengthened, and he used his experience to support and uplift others battling illness, showing how God can turn trials into testimonies of faith and resilience.

4. From Success to Significance: A close friend, once driven solely by career success, found herself empty despite professional achievements. It was during a personal crisis that she sought God's purpose for her life.

She realized that true fulfillment comes from aligning with God's will rather than worldly success. She now mentors others, helping them find their calling and significance in Christ, demonstrating that God's plans surpass our ambitions.

5. Rebuilding After Loss: A fellow believer lost a child tragically and struggled deeply with grief and questioning. Through, a journey of deep sorrow and seeking, they found a renewed purpose in helping others navigate their grief.

Their story illustrates how, even in the profoundest pain, God's presence can bring healing and a new purpose, allowing them to support others through their darkest hours.

These testimonies reflect different journeys, but they all share a common thread in every struggle and every triumph, God's presence is a constant and transforming force. Whether you have had a defining moment or are still waiting for one, remember that God is at work in your life, and the lives of, those around you. Your story is part of a greater narrative and you, are never alone on this journey.

These stories are not just, about what others have endured but also about the hope and strength available to all of us. remember that God's love and power are evident in every story, and He is ready to guide you through whatever comes next.

You are not alone. God is with you, and through every storm, He is shaping, you for something greater. Embrace His presence, draw strength from these testimonies, and continue to seek Him with all your heart. Your story, too, is a testament to His faithfulness.

We are so deeply loved by God. He never changes, and He keeps every promise. Through Him, we find the security and joy of salvation a gift not just for you or me, but for all who come to Him with a heart of full surrender. This surrender becomes a stepping stone that moves mountains, clears paths we never thought possible, and brings us closer to His purpose for our lives.

When we give ourselves fully to God, we start to see the world with a new perspective, through eyes of love, and with a heart like His. Our thoughts shift, our steps are guided by His hand, and we embrace a life, that is continually renewed from beginning to end by His grace. Ask yourself: Are you ready for a new life? A fresh start? The life God has prepared for you?

It doesn't matter how long you have walked with Him or if you are beginning. There is always an opportunity for a reset, a restart, or a renewal. Today is the perfect day to reignite that fire deep within your soul, to let it burn brightly from your heart. Are you ready to discover the new you, the one God has been preparing all along?

Everyone can benefit from a fresh start, and that begins with turning to the One who gives us breath, who breathes life into our days, minds, and souls, and who touches our hearts with a love like never before. So dig deep and keep moving forward. Everyone has a story, testimony, and past but what matters most is how you walk into your future and who you choose to carry with you on that journey.

Are you ready to carry Him with you?

Think about your circle your family, church, work, friends. Every single thing you do in your day matters, even the quiet, unseen things. The choices you make when no one is watching still matter. God sees and knows it all. He tries to protect us, guide us, and reach us by sending His angels to offer comfort, peace, a word, a song, a new hope, a revelation. Sometimes He even gives us a breakthrough, a victory. Yet, too often we are blinded, distracted by this world, pushing God aside with excuses: "I'll come back when I'm ready," "I'm just...," "It will be okay if...," or "God knows my heart."

Yes, God does know your heart. He knows your thoughts even before you think them, and He loves you still. He cares enough to forgive you and gives you time to change and transform within. He gives you the choice to live as you wish, yet He waits with open arms, saying, "I'm here! Come to me, I've got you! Don't worry! You are worthy of my love!" And you are yes, you are worthy of His love.

We know this journey isn't easy. We may stumble, and we may fail Him time and again, but His love is unwavering. He gives us strength to keep moving, to keep growing, to keep seeking, so that we begin to see more of Him and less of our past mistakes. As we look back, we start to see just how far we've come and realize that He truly is the only way. This realization shows Him our love and our true heart.

Remember, knowledge is powerful, but knowing God isn't just about reading His word; it's about drawing near to Him and building a real, intimate relationship. It's about feeling His Spirit, sensing His embrace, not just at your breaking point but also in your victories. Abide with Him daily. Walk with Him, talk with Him, let Him lead you as you follow. Be a living sacrifice, dying daily to your flesh and carnal thoughts. Be a willing vessel for Him, obedient and fully surrendered to our loving Father.

That! Yes, That is what truly matters.

God desires closeness with you. He longs to show you His love, to have a deep, intimate relationship with you not just part of you, but all of you. He wants the "all or nothing." Are you giving Him your all? Are you fully in, holding nothing back? If you feel you're not, there is no better time than now to start. Repent, ask for forgiveness, and move forward in surrender.

14

Conclusion Walking Forward in Faith

I promise that life may still be hard at times sometimes due to our choices but remember, every struggle on this chaotic earth is worth it for the treasures stored in heaven. His love makes it all worth it. He is enough, and He is all we need.

Scripture says:

John 10:10 (NKJV): The thief does not come except to steal, and kill and to destroy *I have come that they may have life and that they may have it more abundantly*

He wants us to have more, much more, but we must let go of our past turn away from what was not from God, and repent, sin separates us from God and his will.

Scripture says:

Romans 3:23 (NKJV): *For all have sinned and fall short of the glory of God.*

Many people try to bridge the gap between themselves and God by doing many good things, but what truly matters to Him is our full surrender connecting our hearts and lives to Him in a deep, genuine relationship. It's about becoming a living, breathing sacrifice, dying daily to our old ways to live in the Spirit He gives us. That's what reaches God. His bridge to us was the cross.

We meet Him there, not by our works, but through the complete surrender of our hearts by our faith.

Scripture says:

John 14:6 (NKJV): *Jesus said to him, I am the way, the truth, and the life, no one comes to the Father except through me.*

Jesus is the only way! Not this world or anything in it, it is Jesus! We must trust him and receive him believe in him and become Children of God.

Scripture says:

Romans 10:9-10 (NKJV): *that if you confess with your mouth* *the Lord Jesus and Believe in your heart that God has raised him from the dead, you will be saved. For with the heart one believers unto righteousness and with the mouth, confession is made unto salvation.*

If you have not received Jesus Christ yet, you can do it right now, right where you are. You don't have to wait for what seems like the perfect moment or when you feel ready; His timing is always perfect, and His invitation is now!

And if you've already received Him but feel the need for a fresh start or a renewal in your spirit, that too, can happen right here, right now. Listen to where God is leading you. This isn't about the people around you, the opinions of others, or making a show of your faith. Yes, we want others to celebrate with us, but it cannot just be about the celebration or the crowd.

It has to be about the intimate relationship between you and God. When we seek Him one-on-one, our eyes open to the wonders of heaven, and we start to see His steps laid out before us, guiding us daily. It's, through these personal moments of connection with our Father, that our spiritual eyes are opened, and we begin to understand His ways more clearly.

So whether it's your first step or a step back into His arms, know that the time is now, and His love is ready to meet you exactly where you are.

So today go to God and admit you need him, let him know you are a sinner.

And repent all to him turn away from the old person, believe that Jesus Christ died for you and me on the cross and rose again ask him to come into your heart pray to him telling him;

Dear God, I know I am a sinner I want to turn away from my sins I ask for your forgiveness I believe that Jesus Christ your son has died for my sins and you raised him to life I want you to come into my heart, and take control of my life I trust you Jesus as my savior and will follow you from this day forward all the days of my life, wash me of all my sins and make me clean, make me whole again, set me free, fill me with the holy spirit help me to see as you see, help me to walk into the new, leaving everything else at your feet in your mighty name Jesus I pray amen and amen.

When you take that step of faith, you walk into the new life God has prepared for you. Each day becomes an opportunity to seek Him more, to desire the fullness He wants for you. This journey may not always be easy, but it is the most worthwhile path you will ever take. It's not just a blessing for you but for generations to come, guided by the One who loved you first with every breath you take.

Remember the great sacrifice He made so you could have that breath the cost was His blood, poured out for you and me. When you wake up each morning, let the memory of His shed blood be at the forefront of your thoughts. Look deep within your heart,

116

and feel the presence of the One who dwells within you. Allow Him to grow within you, to become all-encompassing no more of you, but only His Spirit, His thoughts, His heart.

When we align ourselves fully with Him, our lives are no longer ours alone; it's His Spirit living in us. All we do is prepare the way for Him to come in, recognizing the need for submission and the obedience that full surrender requires. We invite Him in and ask for His will to be done. That is the essence of stepping into a new faith knowing that Jesus intercedes for us daily with strength greater than we can imagine It all begins with that leap of faith, that first step, knowing who leads you, walks beside you, and stands behind you so you never feel alone.

This is the foundation of faith and trust letting Him guide you, day by day, with the assurance with God, all things are possible.

I know it may feel daunting, maybe even impossible but it is entirely within your reach. As you grow closer to God, you will gain a new perspective on your life. The things that once broke you, the storms and struggles that seemed insurmountable may still come your way, and they may be even greater than what you've faced ever. But you will experience a peace like never before a peace that doesn't come from understanding the storm but from knowing who stands with you in the midst of it.

Some may find it hard to grasp this concept, but I promise, you will come to understand. Yes, there will be moments when it feels too hard to bear, but then God steps in, and with Him comes change. You find yourself standing in front of those storms with newfound strength knowing that this time they will not defeat you. Even if you stumble, you will not remain down.

Remember, everything is in His name, there is power in His name revelation, salvation, healing, and transformation. You are born again because of the One who shed His blood to set you free. And that freedom is complete no bondage, chains, generational curses, nothing of your old self nothing of this world can hold you back. It is just His Holy Spirit and your connection to your loving Father.

That's where true salvation lies a full and abundant salvation that comes through complete surrender, obedience, focus, abiding in Him, and living in the truth of God and His Word. With this surrender comes the power to face any storm, not in your strength, or authority but in His. So step forward, knowing that He has already won, the victory for you.

God saves us and then He frees us through the power of salvation. When we believe in Him, He saves us from our old ways, making us a new creation. This is where the true change begins the Holy Spirit ignites new desires within us, guiding us as we take every step in our walk with Him, learning to live out our faith day by day.

Have you begun this journey? If not, I hope that by the end of this book, you will feel inspired to be set free, to leave behind anything that was never meant for your mind, body, and spirit. As you move forward you'll grow stronger, embracing the promises that, come with salvation: freedom, rebirth, full restoration, renewal, fulfillment, healing, and a deeper connection with your loving Father.

Remember, He keeps every promise. Trust that His ways are better, His will is greater, and His timings are always perfect. Let this be the start of your journey toward everything God has planned for you.

Surrender your whole life all in!

Now is the time for God's favor take a step today to salvation!

Walk to your Salvation!

15

Resources:

References and scripture are taken from THE HOLY BIBLE,
  NEW KING JAMES VERSION (NKJV) copyright 1982 by
  Thomas Nelson, inc. Used by permission.
  All rights reserved.

16

Table of Contents Reflection

1. Introduction: The Call to a Transformed Life

– **Understanding True Surrender**
  – **Embracing the Journey of Faith**

2. Discovering Your Defining Moment

– **What is a Defining Moment?**
  – **Questions for Reflection: Finding Your Turning Point**
  – **Testimonies of Change: Stories from Fellow Believers**

3. Understanding God's Love and Purpose

– **Experiencing God's Unchanging Love**
  – **The Purpose Behind Salvation: God's Plan for You**
  – **Living as a New Creation: The Joy of Salvation**

4. The Power of Full Surrender

- What Does It Mean to Fully Surrender to God?
  - Steps to Surrender: Trusting and Letting Go
  - Moving Beyond Fear: Embracing God's Plan

5. Walking with God Daily

- Daily Practices for Spiritual Growth
  - Aligning Your Heart with His: Prayer and Reflection
  - The Role of the Holy Spirit: Our Comforter and Guide

6. Navigating Life's Challenges with Faith

- Facing Storms and Struggles: Finding Peace in the Midst
  - Overcoming Fear and Doubt Through God's Promises
  - The Power of Praise: Celebrating in All Seasons

7. Transformation Through the Word

- The Importance of Scripture: God's Love Letters to Us
  - Living Out the Word: Putting Faith into Action
  - Experiencing Joy Through Spiritual Renewal

8. Building a Closer Relationship with God

- Beyond Religion: Cultivating a True Relationship with God
  - Drawing Near to God: Feeling His Presence Daily
  - The Power of Repentance: Restoring Fellowship with the Father

9. Freedom Through Christ

- Breaking Free from Bondage: Understanding True Freedom
    - Living Beyond Past Failures: Embracing a New Identity
    - Walking in Victory: The Authority of Christ in Us

10. Finding Purpose and Direction

- Discovering God's Plan for Your Life
    - The Role of Faith in Every Decision
    - Moving Forward with Confidence in His Will

11. The Joy of Fellowship and Community

- Growing Together: The Importance of Spiritual Family
    - Sharing Experiences: Encouragement Through Testimony
    - Building Connections that Strengthen Faith

12. Living Set Apart for God

- Understanding Holiness: Being in the World but Not of It
    - Reflecting God's Light: Becoming a Living Witness
    - Choosing Daily to Follow Him: A Lifelong Commitment

13. Preparing for Spiritual Battle

- Equipping Yourself: The Armor of God
    - Standing Firm Against the Enemy: Faith as Your Shield
    - Trusting in God's Timing: Knowing He Fights for You

14. Embracing Daily Renewal and Growth

- The Need for Constant Renewal: Resetting Your Heart and
Mind
    - Seeking God's Will in Every Situation
    - Letting Go of the Old, Embracing the New

15. Conclusion: Walking Forward in Faith

- Reflecting on Your Journey: What's Next?
    - Holding Fast to Hope: Anchored in His Love
    - Committing to Growth: Continuing in His Grace

Made in the USA
Monee, IL
05 March 2025

13537140R00075